MOTORBOOKS COLORTECH

# INSIDE BOEING:
# BUILDING THE 777

BOEING 777

MBI Publishing Company

First published in 2002 by MBI Publishing Company, Galtier Plaza, Suite 200, 380 Jackson Street, St. Paul, MN 55101-3885 USA

MBI Publishing Company books are also available at discounts in bulk quantity for industrial or sales-promotional use. For details write to Special Sales Manager at Motorbooks International Wholesalers & Distributors, Galtier Plaza, Suite 200, 380 Jackson Street, St. Paul, MN 55101-3885 USA.

Library of Congress Cataloging-in-Publication Data Available

ISBN 0-7603-1251-6

Edited by Sara Perfetti
Designed by Katie Sonmor

Printed in Hong Kong

**On the front cover:** The first Boeing 777-300, seen here with a THAI 777-200 in the background, nears final assembly on the floor at Everett in September 1997.

**On the frontispiece:** The 777 cockpit.

**On the title page:** The first Boeing 777 (N7771) is seen here over the Cascade Range near Mount Rainier during a 1995 test flight. By the end of 1995, a nine-ship test fleet had completed 2,451 flights, logging nearly 5,000 hours of test flying. The purpose of the later test flights was to thoroughly evaluate the various engine options.

**On the back cover: Left:** The cool, faint blue light that bathed the first 777 at her debut exploded into kleig-light white as the crowd was allowed to surge forward and swarm around her. As was typical at Boeing roll outs over the previous half century, most of the people in the crowd of nearly 100,000 on hand for the April 9, 1994 event were Boeing employees. **Right, top:** In September 1997, workers at the Boeing Commercial Airplane Group factory in Everett joined the fuselage section for the 100th Model 777. **Right, bottom:** A Lockheed T-33 chase plane zips overhead as John Cashman and Ken Higgins set the prototype 777 (N7771) down at Paine Field at the end of a successful first flight.

# CONTENTS

# HOW DO PEOPLE WANT TO FLY?

On October 15, 1990, representatives from Boeing and United Airlines agreed in Chicago to "design, produce and introduce . . . a truly great airplane . . . that exceeds the expectations of flight crews, cabin crews, and maintenance and support teams and ultimately our passengers and shippers."

They conceived this aircraft in response to market demand for a plane that was larger than Boeing's existing 767 family, yet smaller than the massive 747-400. It was decided that from day one the new aircraft would achieve (a) The "best dispatch reliability in the industry"; (b) "The greatest customer appeal in the industry"; and that it would be (c) "User friendly and [an airplane in which] everything works."

This formally launched the aircraft that will be the primary focus of this book—the Boeing 777, typically referred to as "the Triple-Seven."

United Airlines was Boeing's "launch customer," the customer whose initial order was sufficient for the plane maker to invest the resources to produce the aircraft. By the time the 777 made its first flight in 1994, United had placed orders for 34 aircraft, with options for another 34. As of the first flight, Boeing had more than 140 firm orders for the aircraft.

In June 2001, as Boeing unveiled the concept for the Sonic Cruiser, a Mach .98 twenty-first-century jetliner, at the Paris Air Show, the company presented a program that featured various speakers and commentators of global cultural trends, including noted futurist and author John Naisbitt. In concluding the program, Boeing Commercial Airplanes President and Chief Executive Officer Alan Mulally said, "This airplane is advanced technology's latest and best answer to the question 'how do people want to fly?' This is the airplane our customers have asked us to concentrate on. They share our view that this new airplane will change the way the world flies as dramatically as did the introduction of the jet age."

He might just as well have said the same thing of the 777 program a decade earlier, or the 747 program a quarter century before that. Indeed, it was a question that had been pondered since men like Bill Boeing and Don Douglas had first cut wood on the earliest commercial aircraft in the formative years of aviation history.

# MARKETING AND ENGINEERING

To understand the evolution of the 777 program as a case study in jetliner development, it is necessary to flash back to four other important junctures in the history of jetliner development. These would be the beginning of jetliners themselves; the decision by the two major first generation jetliner makers—Douglas and Boeing—to start "families" of jetliners; the advent of jumbo jets; and finally, the generation of Boeing jetliners that immediately preceded the 777.

The Lockheed L-1011 TriStar made its first flight from Palmdale, California, on November 16, 1970, with H.B. "Hank" Dees and R.C. Cokely at the controls. Also aboard were G.E. Fisher and R.C. Bray from the engineering department.

## In the Beginning

The history of jet propulsion for aircraft began with the turbojet engine invented by British test pilot Frank (later Sir Frank) Whittle, and evolved through World War II with serious military jet aircraft projects undertaken in Germany, Britain, and the United States. After the war, there was an abrupt increase in demand for air travel, and it was naturally assumed that all of the technological advances that had occurred during World War II would be put to work for peacetime consumers. It was obvious that there would be a jet-propelled airliner. The only questions were when and where.

However, as we will come to see as the case studies unfold on the following pages, developing an airliner is not merely a question of technology. As with any consumer product, the development of jetliners is focused by marketing studies.

Sometimes technology and marketing can be at odds. Both eight-track tapes and compact discs represented a technological improvement over vinyl long-playing phonograph records. A glance around your own home will tell you who won—and who disappeared without a trace. Personal computers were technologically possible many years before they came into being, but the marketing people at the major

Lockheed's L-1011 prototype was retained by the company as a test and demonstration airframe and never sold to a customer for airline operations. After 16 years, it would be cut up and cannibalized for spare parts in August 1986.

technology companies were certain that there was no market for them. It took the two Steves from Apple to put computers on the desktops of regular people. It was IBM's turn to play catch-up.

In the years after World War II, the aviation industry was divided over whether there should be jetliners at all. American plane makers, notably the two that were based in Southern California—Douglas of Long Beach and Lockheed of Burbank— were the world leaders in propliners. They were not certain about the future for jetliners, so they stayed with what they knew and they built bigger propliners.

Plane makers in Britain, meanwhile, decided that a jet-propelled airliner would, if successful, put British industry ahead of the Yanks. The result was the de Havilland DH-106 Comet, which flew into the history books as the world's first jetliner on July 27, 1949. The Comet entered service in 1952. It was seen at first as a curious novelty, but just as it was coming to be taken seriously, disaster struck. There was a series of spectacular and well-publicized fatal crashes, and the phrase "Comet Curse" entered the lexicon. No marketing slogan imaginable could undo that stigma.

The Lockheed L-1011, as seen here in 1970, was similar in both size and configuration to the Douglas DC-10. The two aircraft would make their debut flights less than three months apart.

Of course, those on the engineering side of the industry could see that the "Comet Curse" was a curse on the aircraft and not the concept. Still, it was a good time *not* to be building jetliners.

In the United States, both Douglas and Lockheed were thankful that the curse had not fallen on them—and thankful that they were still making propliners. People wanted to fly,

but they wanted to fly safely. Both Douglas and Lockheed had a momentum going with their respective DC-series and Constellation propliner programs.

Up in Seattle, however, the success being enjoyed in the sunny southland was not being matched at Boeing. Sales of the Boeing Stratocruiser were sluggish by comparison to the Douglas

Introduced in 1980, Lockheed's "Advanced TriStar" was actually the original L-1011 prototype with extended wings and improved Rolls–Royce RB211-524 engines. The Advanced TriStar was the forerunner of the L-100-500 series. Some earlier L-1011s would later be brought up to L-1011-500 standards.

and Lockheed equipment. Boeing decided to take a chance that their marketing people could convince the public to give jetliners another look.

The Boeing Model 367-80 jetliner—known familiarly as the "Dash-Eighty," and the prototype of the Boeing 707—made its first flight on July 15, 1954. During the ensuing flight tests, there were no crashes, only a growing flood of orders for the Model 707 production series. Pan American was the first to put the new Boeing 707-120 jetliner into scheduled service, with a debut flight from New York to Europe on October 26, 1958. Within six weeks, Pan American's 707-120s had carried 12,168 passengers across the North Atlantic, and the airline had leased one of its jetliners to National Airlines for use on its New York to Miami route. The era that had been promised by the Comet had dawned—without the curse.

Meanwhile, Douglas and Lockheed—the erstwhile world leaders in commercial aviation—hesitated. Douglas had announced the decision to proceed with development of its own jetliner, the DC-8, but this announcement would not come until June 1955, nearly a year after the Dash-Eighty made its debut. The DC-8 was built, and it entered service with both Delta Air Lines and United Airlines in September 1959—11 months after the 707-120 had entered service with Pan American and a month after the larger, longer-range 707-320 began service.

In marketing circles, they talk about momentum and they talk about who's the first to reach the market with a new product. Boeing had beat Douglas and had defined itself as the new industry leader. At Lockheed, the marketing people had insisted that both Boeing and Douglas were taking a chance on a questionable market. Lockheed sat out round one, choosing to build no first generation jetliner at all.

## The Families

The first generation jetliners, the Boeing 707 and Douglas DC-8, were designed to fly the high-density, high-profile routes where their great speed could really save passengers time. Counting refueling stops, they had cut travel time on transcontinental and trans-Atlantic flying by more than half. They had also revolutionized air travel like nothing before them. Jetliners were their own best marketing tools. A few years before, people had dreaded jetliners. By the early 1960s, they wanted to fly in nothing else.

The first-generation jetliners accommodated up to about 180 passengers depending on configuration, and this proved to be just about right for those transcontinental and trans-Atlantic routes. However, people were excited about jetliners now, and the Boeing marketing people in Seattle and the Douglas folks in Long Beach sensed a market for smaller jetliners for short and intermediate routes where propliners were still in use. This is when the marketing departments at both Boeing and Douglas decided to start "families" of jetliners.

Boeing's 130-passenger, short range 727-100 made its first flight in February 1963 and entered service with both Eastern Air Lines and United Airlines a year later. In 1965, Boeing announced the new 727-200, which would be 20 feet longer than the 727-100, permitting it to carry as many passengers as a 707. Douglas went the other way, building its DC-9-10, which was in the 100-passenger class. Boeing responded with its 737-100, also in the 100-passenger class.

The competition was on. The first flight of the DC-9-10 came in February 1965, 24 months after that of the Boeing Model 727-100, but 26 months ahead of the Boeing Model 737-100. Douglas had not only designed the DC-9-10 to anchor the small end of its family, but to be a family within the family. A whole series of subtypes of varying lengths was part of the plan from the beginning, and it would continue to unfold for four decades. Every successive variant of the DC-9 would be larger. From the DC-9-20 to the DC-9-80, the fuselage lengths would grow in increments of 15, 6, 8, and 14 feet, so that the DC-9-80 series would be more than 43 feet—or half again—longer than the original DC-9s. The DC-9-30 accommodated up to 115 passengers, the DC-9-40 carried up to 125, and the DC-9-50 had a maximum passenger capacity of 139. The DC-9-80, which became the McDonnell Douglas MD-80, would be a family within a family within a family, offering seating arrangements from 130 to more than 170, depending on variant and configuration.

Boeing would eventually terminate production of both the 707 and the 727, but would turn the 737 into a short-range family within a family. At the turn of the twenty-first century, there would be four 737 variants in production. These would be the 110-to-130-passenger 737-600, the 120-to-150-passenger 737-700, the 160-to-190-passenger 737-800, and the 180-to-190-passenger 737-900. In the meantime, Boeing had acquired

TransWorld Airlines was an expected customer for the Lockheed L-1011 after Howard Hughes made overt promises of orders. When Hughes controlled the airline during the 1950s, he had been Lockheed's best customer for its Constellation. This particular aircraft was delivered on March 9, 1972.

LEFT
With its first Lockheed L-1011 received in February 1973, British Airways was the first non-American customer for that airplane. The use of British-made Rolls-Royce RB211 series engines was a critical factor in Lockheed's making the sale.

Britain's Royal Air Force was not the only military service to operate the Lockheed L-1011, but it was the only service to operate the TriStar in aerial tanker configuration. Nine of these were delivered between April 1979 and August 1980.

McDonnell Douglas and had largely phased out the DC and MD line of commercial jets. The 737 family now offered a choice of aircraft beginning with the 737-600 that addressed the same market strata as all but the smallest jets of the 1960s, while the 737-900 could match the 707 or the DC-8.

With the larger jetliners, it was another story.

### The Jumbo Jet

The idea of building families of related jetliners was readily adapted to smaller aircraft, but the expanding airline market of the 1960s led to the demand for a completely new genre of extremely large aircraft that could accommodate more than twice as many passengers as the first-generation 707s and

15

# SUPERSONIC TRANSPORTS

It had been shown by the early 1960s that jetliners not only flew twice as fast as propliners—they were also immensely popular and successful. Thus, it was naturally extrapolated that a *supersonic* transport (SST) that was twice as fast as a first generation jetliner would also be very popular.

By the early 1960s, the technology existed to build aircraft that went that fast, so it was assumed that a practical supersonic jetliner was within reach. All of the assumptions made in the 1940s about the inevitability of jetliners were replayed in the 1960s with respect to the idea of the SST. It was as though people had forgotten that developing an airliner is not merely a question of technology. As with any consumer product, the development of jetliners is focused by marketing studies. Sometimes technology and marketing can be at odds.

The world's first SST, the Anglo-French Concorde, first flew in March 1969. The American SST, the Boeing 2707, never flew. The government funding necessary to complete such a project was terminated in March 1971. By the time that both British Airways and Air France put commercial variants of the Concorde to work in January 1976, it was clear that the SST concept—certainly the Concorde—was not economically viable. A handful of Concordes were still in service at the beginning of the twenty-first century (albeit with a year-long hiatus after the 2000 Paris crash), but they had never been economically viable the way other jetliners have to be. It was only with the aid of generous government subsidies that they were still flying at all.

Two factors had emerged in the early 1970s that turned the SST concept from the wave of the future to merely the wave of a white elephant's tail. Neither of these factors had been imagined during the 1960s by either the marketing or engineering people. The first was the dramatic and sudden increase in fuel costs that came with the energy crisis of 1974. The second was a groundswell of public opposition to the notion of "sonic booms" that occur as an SST exceeds the sound barrier, routinely rattling windows over populated areas. The latter led to a ban on an SST "going supersonic" over land. The Concorde was suddenly limited to supersonic flights only over the ocean, and because of its limited range, this essentially meant only over the North Atlantic.

Because of these issues, the cancellation of the 2707 program was a long-term blessing for Boeing, but it was a short-term disaster.

Even before the energy crisis, the late 1960s and early 1970s had been a hard time for America's largest plane makers. The recession of 1968–1969, brought about by the Vietnam War, had the entire U.S. economy in trouble. Inflation and rising interest rates meant that a larger proportion of corporate income had to go to servicing debt. Meanwhile, a great deal of the income came from work for which prices had been contracted before the cost of borrowing had increased. Lockheed was teetering on the brink of insolvency and Douglas was in the position of having a large backlog of orders, but the company was in a bind for the short-term money needed to complete the orders. Douglas would not have survived if not for its 1967 merger with McDonnell. At Boeing, many major military programs, such as the B-52 and KC-135, came to an end during this period. Projects such as the 2707 and the C-5 military transport, on which the company had counted, simply vanished. On the commercial side, deliveries of 707s dropped from an annual average of 113 in the late 1960s to 59 in 1969, 19 in 1970, and just 10 in 1971. Total commercial deliveries fell from 679 in 1968 to 215 in 1971 and to just 184 a year later. Boeing's earnings dropped 73 billion dollars in one year and a work force of 105,000 was cut to 38,000. Engineers were seen pumping gas. Former Boeing employees spread across the Northwest like spilled ink, trickling into and seriously affecting job markets as far away as Montana. An oft-quoted phrase of the day was "The last person to leave Seattle should turn off the lights."

The German charter airline LTU (Luft-Technische Union) International Airways acquired its first Lockheed L-1011 on May 26, 1972. LTU's livery was somewhat reminiscent of the livery of TWA.

DC-8s. These would be known in the vernacular of the times as "jumbo jets."

Of course, it should be recalled that before the plane makers decided to make jetliners *bigger*, they flirted with the notion of making them *faster*.

In the late 1960s, Boeing was stretched particularly thin because the company was attempting to make both a bigger jetliner *and* an SST. The bigger jetliner concept, which became the remarkable 747, had its origin in 1964, when the U.S. Air Force invited Lockheed, Douglas, and Boeing to submit designs for a large military transport—which would evolve into the giant C-5. In 1965, Lockheed won the C-5 contract, but Boeing President Bill Allen decided that his company would continue its engineering work and build a new jetliner of unprecedented size.

It has often been said that Allen and his successor, Thornton Arnold "T" Wilson, "bet the company" on the 747, and that is true insofar as a failure on so big a project during a major recession would have put Boeing out of business. In retrospect, however, it was a good bet.

From an engineering point of view, no jetliner of the size imagined by Boeing had yet been built, but the C-5 engineering work showed that it was possible.

From the marketing side, meanwhile, an equally promising picture was emerging. Boeing investigators went abroad to examine the airline industry in Europe, Japan, and Australia. They determined that the growing demand for air travel would make a 350-to-400-passenger jetliner viable—if not *essential*—on high-density intercontinental routes by the mid-1970s. The die was cast as the marketing people passed the ball back to the engineering folks.

Early in 1966, Pan American World Airways expressed a commitment to acquire 25 of the proposed 350-to-400-passenger jetliners, and Boeing embarked on the 747 program. Joe Sutter, an engineer who helped develop the 737, became chief project engineer. Boeing purchased a large tract of land adjacent to Paine Field in Everett, Washington, about an hour's drive north of Seattle. It would be here that Boeing would build the vast factory complex to manufacture not only the 747, but the 767 and eventually the 777.

The design and appearance of the new aircraft were discussed and finalized. At first, a stretched 707 was considered, but the idea was abandoned in favor of a number of all-new concepts. These included several variations on a double-decked aircraft about the size of a 707, as well as a much larger jetliner the size of the C-5. In theory, a larger overall aircraft was preferable, but there was concern that a larger plane would not be able to use existing airports. These fears were allayed when the engineers showed that the improved leading-edge and trailing-edge flaps that were a result of the C-5 engineering studies would make it possible for such an aircraft to use existing runways around the world.

The exact width of the new aircraft was a marketing decision that was based on, of all things, the burgeoning market for airfreight. Boeing chose a fuselage width that would comfortably hold two 8x8-foot cargo containers side by side.

The marketing term "widebody" entered the lexicon of commercial aircraft. In terms of passenger capacity, the widebody 747 could carry as many as 500 people—more than twice the number of any other jetliner.

Engines that had been developed by both Pratt & Whitney and General Electric for the C-5 project could be adapted for the 747. Initially, Boeing chose the Pratt & Whitney JT9D turbofan engines to be perfected for the 747.

Saudia (Saudi Arabian Airlines) took delivery of its first Lockheed L1011-200 airliner on May 25, 1975. The Saudi government also purchased L-1011s for official duty as executive transports.

Even as the big production facility at Everett was being built, a network of subcontractors was assembled to provide the components that would flow into it for the 747 program. Because of the unprecedented size of the aircraft and scale of the intended program, the company went to outside suppliers for a larger number of individual subcomponents than it had done for any previous program. This would set a pattern for future programs up to and including the 777.

As with previous Boeing aircraft, a full-scale mockup was constructed to verify engineering drawings, set instruments for flight testing, and check out specific airline cabin and cockpit arrangements—as well as to determine what would be needed within the factory itself in terms of the sizes and configuration of everything from machine tools to the work force.

The largest mockup that Boeing would ever build was finally completed in January 1968, but work was already moving with such momentum that the airframe for the first aircraft itself was completed just eight months later. After the September 1968 roll-out ceremonies, the big aircraft went through an exhaustive

Delivered to Spain's Iberia Airlines on March 20, 1973, this McDonnell Douglas DC-10-30 was later lost in an accident at Boston's Logan Airport on December 17, 1973. During a VFR landing in bad weather, the aircraft clipped a set of approach lights and collided with a dike, which knocked off the right main landing gear. The plane then skidded to a stop. There were no fatalities.

series of tests—from exercising the flight controls to running up the big high-bypass turbofan engines.

The first flight on February 9, 1969 was a well-publicized event, with plenty of news reporters present. The appellation "jumbo jet" was coined, and it would describe not only a new aircraft, but a new era in air travel.

## One Too Many Jumbos?

Well before the Boeing 747 first entered passenger service on Pan American World Airways' North Atlantic route in January 1970, both of Boeing's major competitors had committed themselves to jumbo jets of their own. Boeing had beat them to the punch once before, and neither wanted to be left out of the new generation of jetliners.

ABOVE
The first McDonnell Douglas DC-10-10 ordered by Western Air Lines was delivered as seen here on April 19, 1973, with General Electric CF6-6K engines. The same aircraft was later operated in freighter configuration by Federal Express.

RIGHT
This McDonnell Douglas DC-10-30 was the first of a half dozen such aircraft that were sold to Italy's Alitalia and placed into service between February 6, 1973, and April 19, 1974. It was subsequently operated by Continental Airlines.

PREVIOUS PAGES
This Northwest Airlines Boeing 747-151 was the 27th 747-100 series aircraft off the line at Everett. Powered by Pratt & Whitney JT9D-7A turbofans, it was delivered on April 30, 1970, and photographed over the snow-capped Olympic Range on its delivery flight. The nose section was ultimately preserved for display by the Smithsonian Institution's National Air & Space Museum.

BELOW
Originally operated by United Airlines as a passenger jetliner, this General Electric CF6-6D-powered DC-10-10 was eventually converted to freighter configuration and used by Federal Express. Freighter conversions would be the ultimate fate of many first-generation jumbo jets.

Both Lockheed and Douglas (which became the Douglas Aircraft Company component of the McDonnell Douglas Corporation in 1967) set their sights on the strata of the market that lay between existing jetliners and the 747. Neither the Boeing 707 nor the Douglas DC-8 carried more than about 200 passengers, so there was an obvious gap that centered on a capacity in the 250-to-380 range.

This obvious gap was seen as a market waiting to be filled. With Boeing committed to the 747, the only place in the world where the technology existed to fill the gap was in Southern California.

Having missed the boat entirely a decade earlier, Lockheed was anxious to make up for lost time.

For Douglas, the only way to remain competitive would be to maintain their commitment to a full and comprehensive family of jetliners.

The resulting jumbo jets, the McDonnell Douglas DC-10 and the Lockheed L-1011 TriStar, could not have been more similar. They were both widebody aircraft powered by three high-bypass turbofan engines. They each accommodated 250 to 380 passengers and offered similar performance. They were even within a few feet of having the same dimensions and within 20 percent of having the same gross weights.

The McDonnell Douglas DC-10 and the Lockheed L-1011 TriStar led parallel lives. They were formally announced three months apart in April and July of 1968, and they made their first flights three months apart in August and November 1970—a year and a half after the 747. They were also both built in Southern California—the DC-10 in Long Beach and the TriStar at Lockheed's Palmdale plant out in Antelope Valley. The DC-10 entered service in August 1971, but the L-1011 was not flying paid customers until April 1972. By then, the 747 had been in service for more than two years.

The need for the 250-to-380-passenger jetliner was real, but as we now know—with 20-20 hindsight—the market was not large enough to accommodate two such competing aircraft. Either of the two aircraft would have been immensely successful—but not both. The engineering was sound, but the marketing was much too optimistic. Neither company was willing to be left on the sidelines while Boeing pioneered the jumbo jet genre alone, but they hurt themselves by jumping into the game together.

Both aircraft would remain in production through the 1970s, struggling for market share against the backdrop of higher fuel costs. By the end of the decade, the market was again ripe for new aircraft in the strata of the market below the immense capacity of the 747, but neither McDonnell Douglas nor Lockheed was in a position to exploit it.

Seen here late in its career is a Boeing 747-122 that was originally delivered to United Airlines on May 27, 1971. In the early 1970s, United was still operating with its red, white, and blue livery. The airline would buy 18 747-122s during the early 1970s.

For Lockheed, the L-1011 was the only true jetliner the company ever built, but it would be the last Lockheed commercial aircraft.

McDonnell Douglas would concentrate on its smaller MD-80 series, and not introduce its MD-11—a scaled-up DC-10 with winglets—until 1990.

Up in western Washington, Boeing was ready to accept the new challenge.

# TWO SISTERS SET THE STAGE FOR THE 777

During the 1970s, Boeing emerged as the world's largest commercial aircraft builder. As the decade began, Boeing had bet the company—and won—on the enormous 400-plus-passenger 747 jumbo jet, for which there would be no competitor for the remainder of the century.

Meanwhile, the other two large American plane makers, McDonnell Douglas and Lockheed, had simultaneously entered the market for a 250-plus-passenger jumbo jetliner. As a result, they had effectively neutralized one another through the deleterious war fought between their rival DC-10 and L-1011. If not the most vicious, it had certainly been the most costly fight that anyone in the industry could remember.

By the early 1980s, the impact would be seen and felt. McDonnell Douglas was in decline and Lockheed would announce in December 1981—as everyone had expected—that it would close its L-1011 TriStar production line and abandon the commercial market forever. There was now no doubt as to who was the world's preeminent commercial plane maker, but Boeing would soon have a new competitor.

Ironically, even as McDonnell Douglas and Lockheed were trying to squeeze their respective aircraft into the same narrow niche in the jetliner market, it became evident that there was yet *another* niche in the market that was waiting to be filled. This would be for a 200-plus-seat jetliner. Customers wanted something smaller than the jumbos, but larger than any of the other jetliners then in service. It was into this niche that a newcomer saw a window of opportunity. Enter Airbus Industrie.

Since the late 1950s, the European aircraft industry had gone through numerous cycles of consolidations. Most of the old names had gone, with their expertise now being concentrated into holding

The prototype Boeing 757-200, powered by a pair of Pratt & Whitney PW2037s, is seen here near the time of its debut in February 1982. Never sold to an airline, it was later transferred to Boeing's Logistics Spares component.

The second Boeing 757 ever built was this 757-225, which was delivered to nearly bankrupt Eastern Air Lines with RB211-535E4 engines on August 18, 1983. After the bankruptcy, the airplane was acquired by NASA for use as a "flying laboratory." It is seen here on May 19, 1994, on its delivery flight to NASA's Langley Research Center. It is still in Eastern livery, but the airline's name has been deleted.

companies. By the 1970s, the holding companies would spread across international frontiers to form international consortia. Airbus Industrie was the inheritor of the commercial aircraft traditions of most of Western Europe.

With its final assembly plant in Toulouse, France, Airbus Industrie had been formed in 1970 as a multinational consortium of European aerospace firms—primarily French and German—specifically for the purpose of building a 200-plus-passenger jetliner—the A300. As the decade came to a close, Airbus would emerge as Boeing's only major competition on the world market. This point was made painfully clear to Boeing when Eastern Air Lines abandoned American manufacturers to buy A300s from Airbus. Its A300 was gradually taking the lead in the worldwide market for a jetliner in the twin-aisle 200-plus-seat category.

Meanwhile, McDonnell Douglas had made extensive engineering studies for what they called their Advanced Technology Medium Range (ATMR) aircraft. There was some interest in the proposed aircraft, tentatively designated as DC-11, but not enough to launch the program.

At the same time, Boeing was studying a variety of options. Among these were a 200-plus-seat jetliner and the possibility of forming an international consortium of its own by joining with several Japanese firms to build a new jetliner that was known as 7J7. Cooperation between Boeing and the Japanese aerospace industry had begun in 1969 when Japanese firms had begun participating in the building of Boeing commercial aircraft. Through the years, more than a dozen Japanese companies had been subcontractors, suppliers, or program partners on many Boeing jetliner programs.

In 1978—having considered many options, including the 7J7—the Seattle plane maker answered the challenge of the marketplace with not one but *two* new aircraft. In the usual nomenclature, the next two Boeing aircraft would obviously have to be designated "757" and "767." However, before 1978, nobody knew exactly what these aircraft would actually look like.

Boeing saw that the market was going into the 1980s on a broad front. Of course, there was the 200-plus-seat segment, but there was also a market for a single-aisle 150-plus-seat jetliner. The latter market was then dominated by Boeing's own 727 and McDonnell Douglas's DC-9s, but these airframes were beginning to age, and customers would soon be thinking of replacing them. The 727, with its three-crew flight deck and its three engines, was obviously in need of a more efficient replacement.

The original 757 design, which was being developed as the 727's successor, gradually grew on the drawing board into a 200-passenger aircraft. The second aircraft, designated as the 767, would be the twin-aisle aircraft that would be developed to compete in the 200-plus-seat market. While development of the 757 was actually on a slightly later track than that of the 767, the lower number was assigned to the smaller of the two aircraft for obvious marketing reasons—the bigger plane should have the bigger number!

Meanwhile, with the multinational nature of the Airbus consortium in mind, Boeing took on two international associates as risk-sharing partners in the 767 program. Aeritalia (later Alenia), the largest plane maker in Italy, enlisted in the project on August 14, 1978, and five weeks later they were joined by the Civil Transport Development Corporation of Japan (CTDC), a

Seen here on September 26, 1981, is the first Boeing 767-200. First flown with Pratt & Whitney JT9D-7R4D turbofans, the aircraft was retained by the manufacturer after flight testing and converted for use as the Airborne Surveillance Testbed (AST).

consortium of companies that had been Boeing subcontractors on many earlier projects.

The 757 would emerge as a short- to medium-range jetliner that combined the single-aisle/six across seating typical of the 707, 727, and 737 with new technology wing and engines. The 757 would be capable of carrying about 186 passengers in a typical first class/tourist class configuration, but as many as 220 in an all-tourist configuration.

Eastern Air Lines and British Airways were the first customers for the 757, ordering 40 aircraft between them in August 1978. The formal contract, calling for Rolls-Royce engines, was signed in March 1979, and production began.

## Designing a New Family

Production of the 767 had begun with an order for 30 announced by United Airlines in July 1978. The first 767 (destined to be a Boeing-owned test aircraft) was completed and rolled out of the big plant at Everett in August 1981, and made its first flight on September 26. The first 757 followed its larger sister ship with a debut flight on February 19, 1982.

It was the jetliner "family" concept again. The 757 and 767 shared more than just having made their first flights a few months apart. An important part of the story of their development is how Boeing deliberately designed them to be sister ships. They were designed for two distinct markets, but at the same time they had a great many features in common.

Boeing had planned ahead, knowing that such a feature is an important selling point for airlines that must stock parts for their fleets. Interchangeable parts make for easier and less costly maintenance. In the industry, they call it "commonality."

Commonality was a design principle that had been articulated more than a decade earlier, when Boeing was developing the 727 and the 737—and as Douglas was designing the DC-9. Commonality had been an important factor in both companies' success in keeping customers. A customer who owned 727s had at least one good reason to buy 737s. The two had a great deal in common with one another—and with the 707—especially in their fuselages.

The 757 and 767 were designed with commonality in mind, not only to streamline future maintenance, but current production as well. Though they were not nearly the same size and appeared to be very different, the 757 was described as being "42.8 percent identical" to the 767.

The development of the two new sister ships had represented an intensive effort aimed at refining the design to give maximum fuel performance, operational flexibility, and low noise levels. They were the first all-new jetliners of a new era in commercial aircraft design.

These two jetliners were the first to be developed in the United States since the energy crisis of 1974 altered the way the nations of the industrialized world looked at energy consumption. The most significant change had occurred in Detroit, where carmakers reacted by drastically altering the course of automotive design. The changes for America's plane makers, while less noticeable to the public, were no less dramatic.

Fuel efficiency, a minor concern among first generation jetliners, became an important goal for the 757 and the 767. The goal would be met. For example, on a 500-mile flight the 757 would burn up to 42 percent less fuel per seat than the 727 that it intended to replace. The new wing, fitted with double-slotted trailing-edge flaps and full-span leading-edge slats, would make possible takeoffs with a full passenger load using about 1,250 feet less runway than a 727 taking off on an equal 1,200-mile flight.

With its new wing and high-thrust engines, the 757 would be able to cruise 6,000 feet higher than the 727-200, thus contributing to fuel efficiency, as well as allowing the aircraft to use higher

## A SUPER SALESMAN IN ACTION

By the middle of 1980, orders for the new Boeing 757 were rolling in—with Transbrasil, Air Florida, and Monarch all buying the new bird. Then E.H. "Tex" Boullioun went down to Atlanta to see Delta Air Lines. Tex Boullioun was then the Boeing Company's Senior Vice President for Commercial Airplanes and a member of the seven-member executive council that included the President and the Chairman of the Board of Directors. Tex was also the most successful commercial aircraft salesman in the world. On November 11, 1980, Boeing's "super salesman" closed what was then the biggest commercial aircraft deal in history, selling 60 757s to Delta Air Lines for $3 billion (worth twice that amount in turn of the century dollars). A month later, Delta announced that it wanted its 757s equipped with Pratt & Whitney PW2037 turbofans, giving Boeing's new jet its second engine option. This would greatly enhance the marketability of the 757. For customers who might prefer one engine manufacturer to another, two choices made the aircraft easier to sell!

flight lanes. The four-wheel main landing gear units would allow operations from runways previously unusable by commercial aircraft of equivalent size. Its pavement loading (the ratio of weight-to-surface area) would, in fact, be about the same as the much smaller 737.

At the same time, the 757 and the 767 were the first all-new American jetliners designed against the backdrop of the rising tide of concern over airport noise—as well as new federal noise abatement regulations. The latter would be achieved in large part through the use of a new generation of high-bypass turbofan engines, such as the Pratt & Whitney PW2037 and the General Electric CF6 Series. These were not only quieter than the turbojets that were still common at the world's major airports, they were also much more fuel efficient.

As noted above, the sister ships were 42.8 percent identical. Perhaps the most important feature that the two aircraft had in common was their flight decks. It will be remembered that the late 1970s marked the beginning of the microprocessor revolution that changed so much about our daily lives and the way we think about machines. The Apple II, the first personal computer, was introduced in 1977, even as the 757 and 767 were taking shape on the drawing boards a long day's drive due north of Silicon Valley.

Advanced aircraft systems, including digital electronics, gave the two aircraft the most advanced airliner flight deck ever seen. The old analog "round-dial" flight decks with which the first 707s and DC-8s were equipped were more complex than those of the propliners, but they represented no conceptual advances at all from the instruments of a DC-3. The digital panels of the 757 and 767 flight decks were dramatically different, and it was all due to the breathtaking leap that had occurred in microprocessor technology in the late 1970s. The system that Boeing would adopt centralized all the engine displays for the flight crew, replacing the old electromechanical instruments with high-technology digital electronic equipment.

The two-crewmember flight deck was so highly automated that the pilot and copilot could perform all of their own functions—plus those that the flight engineer would have performed in the old three-crewmember flight deck. The digital system provided automatic monitoring of engine operation and delivered real-time read-outs to the pilot and copilot.

The two-crewmember flight deck was not new in the 757 and 767. Indeed, more than a thousand 737s were already flying with it, but the two sister ships were the first Boeing aircraft whose design originated with a two-person flight crew. Although the elimination of the flight engineer had been unpopular with the unions, it was a development that was simply an inevitable step in the evolution of technology. A similar outcry had occurred a generation earlier when the railroads made the switch from steam to diesel locomotives and began eliminating the firemen from the locomotive cabs.

By making the two flight decks essentially identical, Boeing was expanding its own market. Crewmembers trained and qualified on the 757 could potentially work on the 767 and vice versa. This provided an airline with training benefits and improved crew productivity. If an airline bought a 767 for its routes requiring a 200-plus-passenger aircraft, and later needed a 150-plus-passenger aircraft, where would it look? Obviously, it would look first at the aircraft with a flight deck that was identical to that for which they were already training crew!

Among the innovations that Boeing introduced in the 757/767 flight deck was the Engine Indicating & Crew Alerting System (EICAS). Through graphics and alphanumerics displayed on the center instrument panel on cathode ray tubes (CRTs), the EICAS provided engine operating parameters, caution and warning alerts, and systems status information before takeoff. And for ground personnel, EICAS furnished a readout of electronic systems discrepancies to indicate maintenance requirements.

The flight deck also included an inertial reference system making use of laser gyroscopes that are rigidly fixed to the airliner structure, rather than gyros mounted in gimbals as in earlier airliners. This key system provided information to other flight deck systems, such as the vertical speed indicator and the fuel quantity indicators. Navigation, guidance, and performance data functions were integrated by a flight management computer system. Coupled with the automatic flight control system (the "automatic pilot"), the flight management system provided accurate engine thrust settings and flight path guidance during all phases of the flight from immediately after takeoff to final approach and landing.

The system could predict the speeds and altitudes that would result in the best fuel economy and direct the aircraft to follow the

most fuel-efficient or the "least time" flight path. Depending on the computer programs included, flight planning, ground procedures, and airline route information can be stored for use as required.

The first of the production series 767s (designated as 767-200) was delivered to United Airlines in August 1982, and it carried its first load of paying passengers in September. The first production series 757 (designated as 757-200) was delivered to Eastern Air Lines in December 1982 and made its first revenue passenger flight on New Year's Day 1983. By the end of 1983, there had been 27 757s and 75 767s delivered to customers. Annual deliveries for the next four years averaged 32 for the 757 and 30 for the 767. In 1988, 48 new 757s and 53 767s entered service.

## Planning the Next Step

Meanwhile, Boeing was planning the next step in its jetliner family. This aircraft was obviously going to be designated "777," but nobody—least of all Boeing itself—knew what the 777 would look like.

Indeed, the number would be attached to a number of proposals before it was officially assigned. In the late 1970s, the company had looked seriously at the 777 as a derivative of the 767 idea with approximately the same seating capacity but with a longer, intercontinental range. It was to have been a tri-jet, with the third engine mounted in the tail in a fashion similar to the DC-10 or L-1011. Marketing studies, however, indicated that the company should concentrate on the 757 and 767. The idea of a larger and/or longer-range 767 evolved into the 767-200ER (Extended Range), which first flew in March 1984, and the 767-300, which first flew in January 1986.

As luck would have it, the 1980s would not have been an especially auspicious time for Boeing to have introduced an all-new jetliner. Thanks in part to airline deregulation, the notoriously cyclical airline industry and commercial aircraft industry entered their deepest decline since the 1974 energy crisis.

The years from 1981 to 1984 saw an industry-wide and worldwide decline in new orders. The industry improved somewhat in mid-decade, but by 1986 the industry sales figures had barely crawled back to their 1981 level. Projections for the early 1990s, however, were quite good, as it was predicted that the airlines would then be undertaking the massive task of replacing jetliner fleets, most of which dated back to the 1960s and 1970s.

The clouds were parting. All of the marketing conditions once again were turning favorable. The time was right for Boeing to begin thinking about the aircraft that would become the 777.

This Boeing 767-231ER was delivered to TransWorld Airlines on November 22, 1982, powered by JT9D-7R4D engines. It was TWA's first of ten 767s, delivered over the course of one year and one day. The aircraft was later operated in Africa by Cameroon Airlines.

# A NEW AIRCRAFT TAKES SHAPE

It was in the winter of 1986 that Boeing began to assess the market for an aircraft smaller than the 747 but substantially larger than the 767. It would compete with the Airbus Industrie A300 and serve as a potential replacement for the world's aging fleets of McDonnell Douglas DC-10s and Lockheed L-1011s on transcontinental routes.

Over the course of the next three years, Boeing studied the market as it passed through—and emerged from—a trough on the curve of demand for new jetliners. During this time, Boeing marketing and engineering people consulted formally and informally with major airline customers and bided their time. Finally, it was time to make a decision.

## The 777

In 1989 the company officially formed a "777 Division" within the Boeing Commercial Airplane Group. To head this new organization as its general manager, Chief Executive Officer Frank Shrontz chose 47-year-old Philip M. Condit, who had been an executive vice president responsible for all manufacturing, engineering, product development, customer services, and government technical liaison operations within the Commercial Airplane Group since 1986.

Phil Condit started with Boeing in 1965 as an aerodynamics engineer on the supersonic transport (SST) program, transferred to the 747 program in 1968, and later played a leading role in the development of the 757 program. Between 1978 and 1984 he served as the chief project engineer and as director of 757 engineering. During the ensuing two years he moved across the hall from engineering to marketing, and up the corporate ladder to become vice president for

Released early in 1992, this dramatic rendering was designed to demonstrate that the Boeing *777*—still three years from first flight—would promise the widest cabin in its class. This would translate as four abreast in first class or five in business class. For Economy, nine abreast seating was suggested.

sales and marketing of the Commercial Airplane Group. In 1996 he would succeed Shrontz as CEO (but that is getting ahead of the story).

By 1989 the microprocessor revolution that had begun in the 1970s had evolved dramatically. The 1980s had been characterized by a staggering increase in computer capabilities. Things were possible in 1989 that could not have been imagined in 1978 when Phil Condit went to work on the 757 program. However, what was to happen in the early 1990s would dwarf even what occurred between 1978 and 1989. It will be recalled that in 1989, DOS was still the standard operating system on most computers.

Phil Condit was part of a savvy generation of engineers—*and* marketing people—who understood what had happened and what was continuing to happen in the world of computers. As general manager of the new 777 Division, he made the decision to fully adopt digital technology, not just as something to be attached to the flight deck of a finished airplane, but as something that would be integral to inaugurating an entirely new approach to aircraft design.

Condit and his team reorganized the entire design process. Boeing had used Computer-Aided Design (CAD) and Computer-Aided Manufacturing (CAM) systems before, but the 777 would be the world's first all-digital aircraft.

To make this happen, Boeing would choose the CATIA (Computer-Aided Three-Dimensional Interactive Application) process, developed in France by Dassault Systemes. Marketed in the United States by IBM, CATIA used IBM's UNIX-based RISC System/6000 workstations. Because CATIA operated in three dimensions (see sidebar), there was theoretically no need for Boeing to construct a full-scale mockup of the 777.

Within the automotive industry, companies such as Daimler Benz, BMW, Fiat, Volvo, and Saab had already been designing cars without full-scale mockups, using the process called "virtual prototyping." This had been demonstrated to have resulted in a substantial reduction of development time and manufacturing costs. However, no project as large as a jetliner had ever been designed without a full-scale mockup.

Boeing would be breaking new ground.

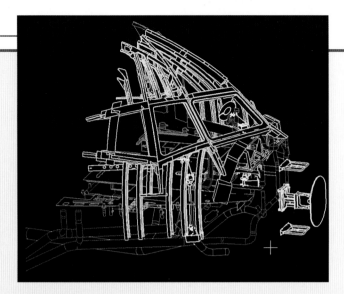

*This image produced via CATIA software shows a "wire-frame" detail view of the starboard side of the 777 flight deck from a slightly elevated angle. The red lines represent flight controls, and the radar system is indicated in white. Using CATIA, designers were able to render, then rotate, such three-dimensional detail drawings, something that was impossible in analog drawings or in two-dimensional CAD applications.*

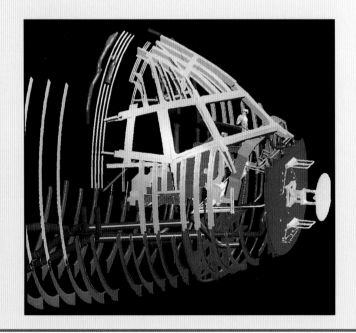

# THE CATIA STORY

The roots of Computer-Aided Design (CAD) and Computer-Aided Manufacturing (CAM) can be traced to the early 1950s, and early computing systems were used throughout the aerospace industry during the 1960s and 1970s. However, they were extremely complex, very expensive, and by today's standards, very slow. This limited their overall effectiveness and practicality. Another factor that greatly limited their usefulness was that CAD/CAM (aka CADAM) software could visualize in only two dimensions. For generations, engineers who did their work with pencil and paper were limited to two dimensions, and early digital applications were based directly on the age-old analog two-dimensional environment.

Engineers designing three-dimensional machines with curved contours and complex angles, such as automobiles and aircraft, had traditionally designed their machines using two-dimensional pen and pencil drawings on Mylar or vellum paper. Because of the problems of interpreting and realizing two-dimensional data, however, they always had to construct both models and full-scale mockups in order to be able to see their creation in three dimensions. The three-dimensional solid images could be rotated and viewed from any angle, as well as studied and positioned within a larger object being assembled.

The demands of aeronautical design had overwhelmed the early CAD/CAM systems, but it would be an aerospace company that would solve the problem. In 1977, Avions Marcel Dassault, the French company responsible for France's leading-edge military aircraft (including the Mirage family of fighters) began work toward developing a three-dimensional CAD/CAM system.

By 1981 the Dassault engineering team had created a system that would be known as CATIA (Computer-Aided Three-Dimensional Interactive Application). It was, as the name implied, a three-dimensional, interactive program capable of using drafting calculations with roots in descriptive plane geometry to render three-dimensional virtual models within the computer.

As the decade unfolded, the speed of computers increased exponentially, and it was possible to render virtual models faster than building actual models. Of course, the real benefit of CATIA was that important structural changes could be rendered quickly and efficiently.

The company created a subsidiary called Dassault Systemes to develop and improve CATIA, and a marketing agreement was signed with IBM. CATIA Version 1, released in 1982, found a ready market throughout the aerospace community in America and Japan, as well as in Europe. By the middle of the decade, CATIA was also being used extensively in the automotive world and for the design of consumer products from ski boots to furniture.

While the early CATIA program worked in conjunction with existing CAD/CAM applications, an upgrade announced in 1984 added surface modeling and drafting capabilities, giving CATIA an internal CAD/CAM capability.

Version 2, introduced in 1985, had fully integrated drafting, as well as solid and robotics functions, and CATIA Version 3, in 1988, had full architecture, engineering, and construction (AEC) functionality. It was here that Boeing entered the picture with the decision to adopt CATIA as the system for designing the first digital aircraft.

CATIA Version 4, announced in 1993, greatly expanded the system's networking potential, by allowing a user to perform several operations concurrently, such as designing in three dimensions, creating engineering drawings, analyzing a product or assembly, viewing it as a rendered image, and speeding up manufacturing processes. Now everyone on the network would have simultaneous access to the same data in a common format and to all updates.

LEFT
*This image produced via CATIA software shows a fully rendered structural view of the starboard side of the 777 flight deck from a slightly elevated angle. The red tubes represent flight controls, and the radar system is indicated in white. The green and yellow sections represent structural components.*

LEFT
Engineers on the 777 program used digital, three-dimensional computer modeling to design components for aircraft such as the 777. Parts could be viewed from any angle, and, as we see in this June 1991 photograph, cross-sections could be easily extracted from solid depictions of the parts.

The sophisticated digital computer workstations developed by Boeing for the 777 program were state of the art in 1991. They had already replaced traditional computer-aided design (CAD) systems. This engineer was working on a fuselage section with systems routings, all of which are depicted as three-dimensional solid images.

The workstations used in the 777 project were equipped with CATIA (Computer-Aided Three-Dimensional Interactive Application) software. This allowed engineers to design and preassemble the aircraft 100 percent digitally. In this January 1992 photograph, these engineers are defining floor structures. CATIA capability greatly improved accuracy, reduced the need for full-scale mockups, and enhanced the overall quality of the airframe.

Boeing had been using computers for three decades and had databases in a myriad of software formats, many of them outmoded by the rapidly evolving state of the art in digital information management. Indeed, many systems in place at Boeing had been developed for the B-29 program during World War II, and had been adapted and readapted for the 700-series jetliners as the jetliners had evolved.

Despite the huge volume of digital information and both software and hardware, Boeing had never attempted anything on this scale previously, nor had any major commercial airframe maker. Some components on earlier Boeing aircraft had been designed and tested digitally, but even as late as the early 1980s, creating something on the scale of an entire jetliner was literally unthinkable.

By 1989 it was obvious that the old way of doing things was on the way out. Condit would organize his engineers into teams focused on specific parts of the aircraft and rethink the way that computer systems were used in the process of designing aircraft.

As is suggested in this 1992 view of Boeing's 777 Division design facility, engineers from multiple disciplines could work on the same section of the design concurrently using the CATIA software. The Division had about 2,000 work stations linked to what was then the world's largest mainframe computer cluster dedicated to a CAD/CAM application.

The entire process was being changed. Once there had been several independent wing design and wing manufacturing groups within the company. After the experience of the 777, Boeing would have just one "wing responsibility center" for all the programs. The same would be true for other aircraft components.

Of course, it was not merely a case of embracing technology for the sake of technology. There was a sound business model at work. Condit's team understood that every new design done the old analog way inevitably resulted in reworking components that simply didn't fit with other components.

Complexity inherent in aircraft is magnified in the art of aircraft production. Airplanes contain millions of parts and subcomponents that require detailed drawings. Eventually, the millions of parts have to be multiplied by hundreds of airframes and by the thousands of physical operations that take place in connecting each part to other parts.

The 777 Division teams recognized that CATIA had the potential to reduce the reworking and cut down drastically on changes. Reworking cost money. Every dollar saved in such a process slipped to the bottom line and added to overall profitability.

Cost savings are always important, but computer-aided systems also had the potential to save time. It is axiomatic that for a product to thrive in the marketplace, the company that manufactures it must be nimble and responsive to the demands of the market. Another way that CATIA would save time is that when the aircraft was ready for FAA certification, complete records of every step in the design and prototyping process would have been recorded.

There was also the practical issue of maintaining a parts inventory during the manufacturing process. All of these parts had to be designed and/or specified, and there would literally be tens of millions of them. With CATIA, however, they would become part of the computer database at the time they were *designed*, and this database could be adapted for inventory management during the production phase. Meanwhile, an exact knowledge of the size and shape of every part was an invaluable aid in manufacturing the tooling that would, in turn, be used to manufacture the parts.

## Going to Work

To simplify the three-dimensional solid modeling for what was to be the world's first all-digital aircraft design, Boeing would install about 1,700 CATIA workstations in the Puget Sound area.

In January 1992 the Electrical Systems Engineering team from Boeing's 777 Division met with United Airlines representative Brandon Maus (fourth from right). For the meeting, designers were able to produce schematic drawings of the systems to be discussed by simply printing out work done inside the CATIA computer network.

These were tied together through several IBM mainframe computers that were centered in Everett. In turn, workstations on the network were parceled among nearly 300 teams, the members of which included people from Boeing's engineering and manufacturing areas—especially in western Washington State, Philadelphia, and Wichita—as well as representatives of major suppliers and major airline customers. Aerospace firms from throughout the United States, as well as in Canada, Europe, and the Pacific Rim, were also involved in the design effort.

The choice of Everett was one of two that the Boeing Commercial Airplane Group could have made. The other would have been Renton, Washington, the location of the headquarters of Boeing Commercial Airplane Group, about a half-hour's drive southeast of Boeing Field in Seattle. Boeing Field, which

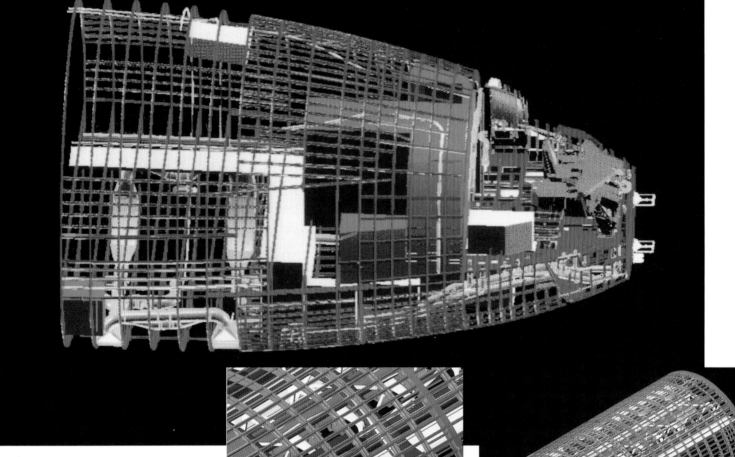

## ABOVE

What appears to be a color photograph of a very complex three-dimensional model is actually a CATIA-rendered drawing of the nose of a 777 in the inverted position. In this upside-down illustration, the green indicates the structure of the aircraft itself, while the turquoise objects represent payload. With CATIA, designers were able to ensure that payload containers would fit precisely.

## BOTTOM LEFT

In this CATIA-rendered three-dimensional detail drawing of a 777 fuselage section, it is evident that the structural area around the windows (shown in green) is "beefed up." The red lines are flight controls. In past years, any revisions done to such a drawing would have required extensive handwork; with CATIA, such a task is now quick and easy.

## BOTTOM RIGHT

The green "strawberry-basket" structures in this CATIA-rendered 777 fuselage section represent the structure of the aircraft itself. Using CATIA, designers on the 777 project could preassemble the aircraft on the computer screen to detect misalignments and other interface problems before costly machine tools were built.

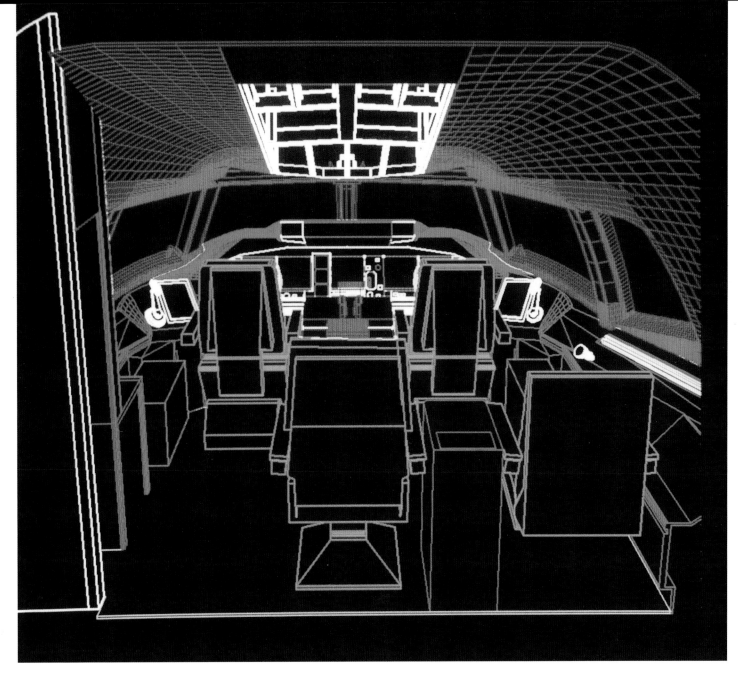

This CATIA-rendered "wire-frame" look at the flight deck of the 777 shows that the eventual configuration was clearly taking shape late in 1991. The red lines indicate the interior structure of the aircraft, while blue is used to show three-dimensional structures within the cabin. The areas rendered in white indicate where controls and flat panel digital displays would be situated.

43

Japan's Mitsubishi Heavy Industries and Kawasaki Heavy Industries were both involved by Boeing in the 777 design process. Seen here conferring on a CATIA-rendered fuselage section are (clockwise from left) Melody Gullege and David Kent of Boeing, Terry Tajima of Kawasaki, and Junji Oki of Mitsubishi. Kengo Hayashi, also of Mitsubishi, is seated at the workstation in the center.

had been the headquarters of the Boeing company from 1916 to 2001 (when the top executives were relocated to Chicago), had seen no large-scale manufacturing since the 1950s. At Renton, Boeing Commercial Airplane Group also maintains its assembly line for its 737 and 757 series aircraft.

Meanwhile, final assembly of the 747 and 767 occurs at the Everett plant north of Seattle that was originally built for the 747 program. Theoretically, the 777 program—including the eventual final assembly—might have been located at either site. Everett was chosen because there is more room for expansion and because Everett has a "large aircraft" specialization.

In July 1991 Boeing would be granted its initial construction permit to begin a major expansion of the Everett facility to support the 777 program. There would be a 50-percent increase in what was already the largest building in the world by volume.

On the software side, Boeing created and customized over 200 digital systems to aid the CATIA-using teams. These included the Finite Element Analysis System, developed in France by Dassault Systemes and, like other Dassault products, licensed in the United States through IBM. Other software included "Electronic Preassembly Integration on CATIA" (EPIC) as well as digital preassembly applications developed by Boeing itself.

Although they would be physically separated by dozens—even thousands—of miles, the teams would all be able to work together in the same "virtual" world. CATIA would not only permit the teams to digitally preassemble the aircraft, but to conduct virtual walk-throughs of preassembled sections that existed only in electronic form. For people used to the old analog way of doing things, it was literally a step into a new world.

Among the major suppliers networked with the Boeing teams was a consortium of several Japanese firms that were investing their own resources in the project, as Japanese firms had done on the 767 program since 1978 through the Civil Transport Development Corporation (CTDC)—later known as the Commercial Airplane Company (CAC). Japanese involvement in the 777 program began in May 1991 with a master 777 program contract being entered into between Boeing and a consortium headed by the Japanese Aircraft Development Corporation (JADC). Under this agreement, the Japanese firms would be responsible for about a fifth of the actual structure of the airframe. The principal Japanese companies involved included Fuji Heavy Industries, Kawasaki Heavy Industries, and Nippon Industries, as well as global industrial giant Mitsubishi Heavy Industries. To be certain that the Japanese companies were fully integrated into the process, a new digital data center was built in Japan. It was not just vital, it was essential that Everett and Japan be working, through CATIA, on identical configurations.

Just to show how far data transmission technology has advanced since 1989, Everett was linked to its Japanese partners through a fiber-optic cable that had recently been laid across the Pacific Ocean rather than via satellite transmission! Today, we take routine satellite communications for granted, but in 1989, it was still a developing technology and the first full flowering of the Internet was a half decade in the future. Indeed, e-mail would not replace faxes as the primary means of internal communication within Boeing itself until around 1997.

By the late 1990s, the implementation of the Microsoft Exchange e-mail system would give Boeing managers a standard communication tool that allowed faster communication and faster decision making. Decisions that previously languished between monthly executive meetings could be made within hours.

## Designing the Future

As they began building their virtual aircraft in their virtual world, the CATIA teams discovered that major changes could be made in hours instead of weeks. Design engineers and manufacturing engineers worked on the design of the same parts simultaneously; this would have the effect of decreasing subsequent change orders.

Digital design would also result in many forms of fine-tuning not previously possible. Building on previous experience with the 757 and 767—as well as earlier analog models—Boeing engineers were able to use CATIA to create a wing with the most aerodynamically efficient airfoil ever developed for subsonic commercial aviation. The 777 wing—spanning an inch shy of 200 feet—would feature increased thickness while allowing the aircraft to climb faster, reach higher cruising speeds, and cruise at higher altitudes than other contemporary jetliners. This would also permit operations with full payloads from high-altitude airports during hot weather.

In the late 1970s, as the 757 and 767 had been taking shape, one of the most important features of the shape that they were taking was in the area of materials technology. Throughout the global aviation industry, embedded carbon fibers, resins, and other composite materials were coming into use as a lighter-weight replacement for aluminum in many aircraft structures. Aircraft are designed with a weight budget in mind, and weight savings are sought wherever possible without compromising safety.

This trend toward composites would continue to play out in the development of the 777. Indeed, non-metal materials would account for nine percent of the new aircraft's structural weight, compared to about three percent on other Boeing jetliners. The

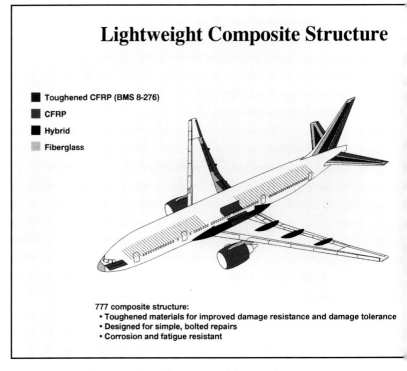

## Lightweight Composite Structure

- Toughened CFRP (BMS 8-276)
- CFRP
- Hybrid
- Fiberglass

777 composite structure:
- Toughened materials for improved damage resistance and damage tolerance
- Designed for simple, bolted repairs
- Corrosion and fatigue resistant

This April 1993 illustration shows the portions of the 777 that were composed of lightweight composite materials. Indeed, nine percent of the aircraft's structural weight was composites. Boeing had used composites in the structure of previous aircraft, such as the 767, but never as much as in the 777. The green areas indicate Carbon Fiber Reinforced Plastic (CFRP), the red areas "toughened" CFRP, and the pale blue areas were fiberglass.

areas utilizing carbon fiber materials included tail surfaces, floor beams of the passenger cabin, and aerodynamic fairings.

In addition to composites, an improved aluminum alloy known as "7055" would be used in the upper wing skin and stringers. This material offered greater compression strength than other alloys then in use. It also offered improved corrosion and fatigue resistance along with a savings in weight.

In the course of designing any commercial aircraft, one of the guiding principles is airport compatibility. As much as designers would often like to think outside the box, a new aircraft must fit within the "box"; that is, it must fit within the parameters of

In the interest of airport compatibility, Boeing originally proposed the 777 with optional folding wingtips. As can be seen in this July 1991 illustration, the feature would have permitted three 777s to use a section of a terminal that could otherwise be served by just two aircraft of this size. The hydraulically actuated system would have folded the outboard 21-feet 3-inch sections upward. No airline ordered the feature so it was dropped.

the airports that it serves. Jetliners are required to be adaptable to fixed airport equipment, such as airport arrival and departure gates. It's obvious that smaller aircraft can be accommodated at more gates in the same given space than larger aircraft.

In 1991 designers proposed a unique method of adapting the 777 to fit existing 757/767 gates. Their suggestion was optional folding wingtips. A hydraulically actuated system was designed to fold the outboard 21-foot wing sections upward, reducing overall wingspan to just over 155 feet, which was about the same as a 767. Such a feature would allow three 777s into a space that would otherwise accommodate just two.

The main landing gear for both the 757 and 767 had been the conventional two-post configuration with standard four-wheel trucks, for a total of eight, plus two wheels in the nose gear. For the heavier 777, Boeing engineers used the standard two-post arrangement, but with six-wheel trucks, the largest ever incorporated into a commercial aircraft. The 12 wheels permitted superior weight distribution on runways and taxi areas as well as a more efficient braking system. The larger 747 has a 12-wheel arrangement, but it is a combination of four-wheel trucks and complementary two-wheel gear under the center of the fuselage. Another advantage is that the six-wheel trucks allow for a more economical brake design.

When a new aircraft program is initiated by a plane maker, it is traditional to assign a test pilot from the manufacturer's flight department as the program's chief pilot. With the 777 program, Boeing went a step further and created the role of chief mechanic for the program. As with the chief pilot, the chief mechanic was intended to become the advocate for all the mechanics at the airlines and repair stations who would encounter the 777. The creation of the chief mechanic position was out of the acknowledgment that the maintenance side of aircraft operations, like the operational side, reinforces an airline's success in terms of both safety and scheduling.

Among the factors studied by the chief mechanic were such things as access and visibility. One simple example might be when a mechanic must turn a valve from an unwieldy position, to ask whether the force necessary is within the mechanic's capability in this position. Other things might include making sure that a mechanic has sufficient visibility in a particular area if the work has to be done at night or in bad weather.

In order to be certain that the design of the 777 would address market needs and customer preferences, Boeing brought several key airline customers into the process at an early stage. These airlines included United Airlines, British Airways, and Hong Kong's Cathay Pacific, as well as two Japanese carriers, All Nippon Airways and Japan Airlines. Among them, they represented a broad spectrum of route structures, traffic loads, and service frequencies.

There would be intensive dialogue and hours of meetings as the customers and suppliers worked with Boeing to define the ultimate configuration of the new aircraft. Customer input early in the design process was intended to aid Boeing in building a plane that would satisfy a broad spectrum of customers with differing route structures, traffic loads, and service frequencies.

During the course of the meetings, it was decided that many features that had typically been offered as optional, would be standard on the 777. Just as radios and air conditioning were once optional equipment that are now standard in automobiles, nearly a hundred features became standard on the 777 for the first time in a major new jetliner. These included satellite communication capability and a Global Positioning System (GPS) for the flight crew and a state-of-the-art digital sound system for the passengers.

## The Passenger Cabin

The airline customers were also pleased to be involved in creating what turned out to be one of the most flexible passenger cabins ever developed. It was designed and fine-tuned on CATIA; then, in 1992, a full-scale interior mockup was constructed at Renton, using actual seats that people could sit in, as well as fasten their seatbelts and lower their tray tables.

Customers—both current and potential—could come to Renton, walk through a door in an office building, and find themselves in the cabin of a jetliner that would not exist for another three years. They could walk through an economy section that could be configured for nine or ten abreast, and move forward into

Economy-class seating in the 777 was designed to accommodate a ten-abreast, high-density maximum. With an interior cross-section of 19 feet 3 inches, the aircraft had the widest interior of any jetliner in its class. The seats that are shown in the arrangement seen here are identical to those that were already being used aboard the Boeing 757 and the company's 737 family.

While the interior cross-section of the 777 cabin was designed to accommodate a ten-abreast configuration, the nine-abreast layout seen here allows a bit more room. The 2-5-2 arrangement is always preferred over the 3-4-3 layout by passengers sitting in window seats—and by those seated next to them. Boeing's idea was to allow enough space to give their airline customers many seating options.

RIGHT
This cut-away rendering illustrates a 777-200 with a tri-class configuration that includes four rows of first class and two of business class. Also of interest here is a depiction of the optional folding wingtip feature that was originally proposed, but later deleted from the design. The 777 wing was described as the most efficient airfoil yet developed for a subsonic commercial aircraft.

In this view of the 777 first class cabin mockup, Boeing employees and potential passengers relax in the famous 777 "sleeper seats." The two men in the first row obviously have plenty of legroom. The first-class cabin was also designed to have greater headroom and straighter sidewalls than competing jetliners in its class. Boeing also advertised enhanced lighting.

In this photograph of the 777 cabin, seven-abreast business-class seating is seen in the foreground, and nine-abreast economy seating is shown aft. The man who is standing is six feet two inches tall and clearly would have plenty of headroom in business class, as well as in economy. Meanwhile, the five-foot four-inch woman in the background is apparently retrieving her bag from the overhead bin with relative ease.

a five-abreast business class and a four-abreast first-class cabin.

The interior wiring, plumbing, and attachment fixtures had been designed to accommodate "flexibility zones" located specifically in the vicinity of the aircraft doors. Within these zones, galleys and lavatories could be positioned or repositioned anywhere within one-inch increments. In addition, overhead compartments were designed for quick removal without disturbing ceiling panels, air conditioning ducts, or other structures. The interiors were designed so that reconfiguration of an entire cabin could be accomplished in three days rather than the several weeks required in other aircraft.

Below the cabin floor, the 5,656-cubic foot lower hold was designed with a mechanized cargo-handling system that would be compatible with any unit-load devices or pallet types then in use aboard passenger aircraft. Specifically, the hold was designed to accommodate 32 standard LD-3 containers, as well as 600 cubic feet of bulk cargo.

In June 1992 the 777 passenger cabin would win the Industrial Designers Society of America Award for Design Excellence. It was the first time that an aircraft interior was awarded this honor. A year later, in June 1993, the 777 flight deck would capture the same award.

## The Flight Deck

For three decades, Boeing had been involving "human factors specialists," many of whom were also pilots or mechanics, in flight deck design. Indeed, an outside team of senior human factors specialists took part in 777 flight deck design reviews early in the program. They studied such factors as human performance, physiology, visual perception, ergonomics, and the interaction between people and computers. The objective has been to improve safety as well as reliability and crew comfort.

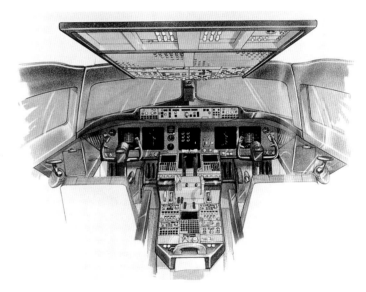

As can be seen in this artist's drawing, the all-digital, "glass-panel" flight deck of the 777-200 was a step beyond the old-fashioned "round-dial" environment of the flight decks of past-generation jetliners. Similar to the popular, all-digital, horizontal flight deck of the 747-400, the 777 flight deck was designed to optimize the flight crew's situational awareness, minimize "head-down" time, and accommodate current and future avionics technology.

Although the 777 is much larger than late-model 767s, its flight decks share roughly the same layout. In this view, Captain John Cashman (left), 777 Program chief pilot, grasps the throttle levers, while 777 Project Pilot Captain Frank Santoni watches from the first officer's seat. The 777 flight deck was designed with flat-panel displays, fly-by-wire flight controls, color flight management computer control display units, and cursor controls that function like a personal computer mouse at the touch of a fingertip.

During the 1970s and 1980s it was discovered that more reliable flight deck designs helped reduce the accident rate and increase efficiency—although advancement in engines, systems, and structures also had contributed to this result.

At the start of the 777 design process, airline flight crews and mechanics worked with Boeing design teams on all aircraft systems. Eleven of the first customers also took part in flight deck design reviews early in the process. Airline customer crews would be invited to spend time in the 777 engineering flight simulator to assess the layout in a variety of normal and unusual situations and scenarios.

Airline customer flight crews favored a horizontal flight deck layout similar to that which was then being installed in the 747-400. First delivered in 1989—two decades after the introduction of the classic 747—the 747-400 represented the leading technological edge among Boeing jetliners at the time that the 777 was being defined. Certainly, the 747-400 flight deck was state-of-the-art for the early 1990s.

On the flight deck that was selected for the 777, large advanced liquid crystal display (LCD) screens provide the flight crew with real-time engine, flight, and navigation data. These flat-panel displays are much lighter, thinner, and more reliable than the TV screen-style cathode ray tube (CRT) screens that had replaced analog round-dial panels in the 757/767 generation of jetliners. They also draw less power and offer a great deal of weight savings. Not only are they lighter than the CRTs with their heavy glass screens, the flat panels generate less heat, and therefore don't require the heavy and cumbersome cooling equipment installed for the CRTs.

The flat panel displays are also favored because they are brighter and more readable. Unlike CRTs, they remain clearly visible even in direct sunlight. Contributing to their readability is the fact that the flat panels incorporated into the 777 flight deck display in full color. Pilots specifically requested this feature because data displayed in different colors can be more quickly assimilated. To put this into historic context, it should be recalled that the development of the 777 during the early 1990s coincided with the shift from monochrome to full color computer monitors in homes and offices.

Both the captain and first officer would have LCDs directly in front of them that would display essential data such as air speed, altitude, compass heading, pitch, rate of climb, and roll attitude. Between them in the center would be the three flat panels of the multipurpose Control Display Units (CDUs). Visible to both the captain and first officer, these would furnish information related to flight management functions that is processed and presented by the integrated Airplane Information Management System (AIMS).

Boeing had contracted with Honeywell and Sundstrand to develop the primary 777 flight control systems, including AIMS and the Air Data/Inertial Reference System. These embedded systems were designed using the real-time programming language ADA (not an acronym, but a standard computer software language named after Lady Ada Augusta Byron). Honeywell's AIMS would have 15,656 kilobytes of disk space and 4,854 kilobytes of random-access memory (RAM).

AIMS would also include the central maintenance function, which gathers data from other aircraft computers. The data would then be displayed to the flight crew so that they could take action related to potential hazards—such as an impending engine failure. Routine maintenance data could also be stored for preparation of repair logs for ground crews.

By the early 1990s, three-axis "fly-by-wire" flight-control systems had long since replaced steel cable mechanical systems. The captain and first officer would fly the aircraft with this system by relaying maneuvering directives directly to hydraulic actuators by way of 11 pathways of ARINC-629 electrical wires. The actuators control the flaps, ailerons, elevators, rudder, and other control surfaces. ARINC-629 allows systems and computers to interface through a common twisted pair of wires instead of through separate one-way wire connections. This system simplifies assembly while increasing reliability by reducing the volume of wiring within the aircraft. Patented by Boeing,

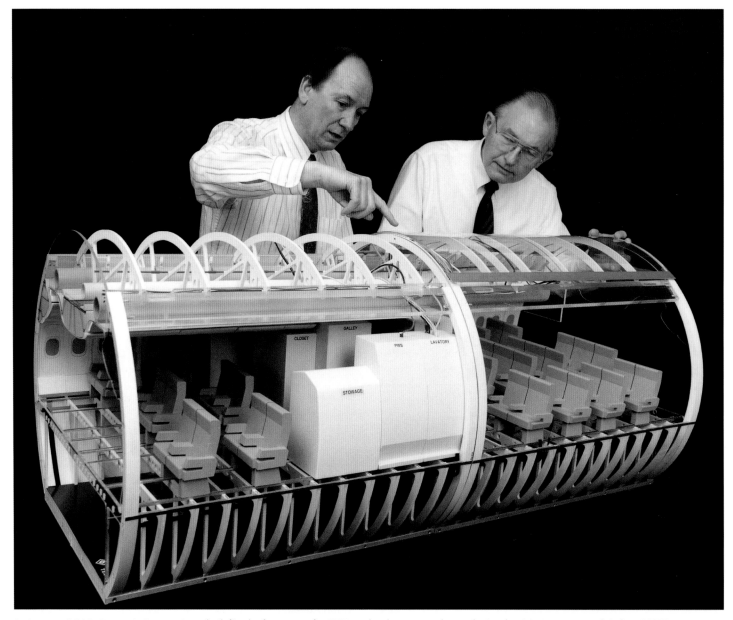

In January 1992, Boeing's George Broady (left), chief engineer for 777 payloads, got together with Gordon McKinzie, United Airlines' 777 program manager, to discuss the flexibility of internal features. As can be seen in this 10th-scale model of a fuselage section, modular galleys, lavatories, and stowage units—like seats—were attached to tracks so that they could be easily repositioned within pre-engineered "flexibility zones."

ARINC-629 would become an industry standard by the end of the 1990s.

In the fly-by-wire aircraft, it is not necessary for control devices such as the yoke and column to move, as they do in aircraft with traditional controls. However, it has been shown that tactile motion cues reinforce awareness and help to keep a flight crew fully focused on changes occurring to flight status and flight path. Both control yokes and columns in the 777 turn together when either is moved, so that the control input of each flight crewmember is immediately obvious to the other.

Thanks to the virtual prototyping capabilities of CATIA, representative pilots from the customer airlines could actually "tour" the flight decks before any metal was cut, and make suggestions and recommendations to the designers. As they worked, the design teams were actually creating more than just a digital aircraft mockup. A byproduct of their work was that they were creating within CATIA a vast database of product information. Indeed, all of the data needed to manufacture and ultimately to maintain the 777 was in the foundation that was being constructed in their virtual world.

## PLANNING AHEAD

An important aspect of the flight deck design that was not immediately apparent in a walk-through was the attempt by designers to create an environment that could evolve and adapt to change. In less than a generation, aircraft designers had watched the evolution of flight deck avionics from analog to digital, and from CRT to flat screen.

Things were changing even as they designed the flight deck—and more changes could already be visualized for the near future. With this in mind, it was imperative that the control panels of the flight deck be laid out in such a way that it could be retrofitted with both expected and unanticipated future avionics and other flight deck features.

Certainly in the categories of "other" and "unanticipated" would be the flight deck security measures that would be introduced after September 11, 2001.

### Designing With the Competition In Mind

At some point during the cabin tour described above, Boeing staff would remind customers and potential customers that the 777 cabin would be the widest in its class. As Boeing engineers and their counterparts in Japan well knew, this class would include the Airbus Industrie A330 and A340 that were, at that moment, being developed in Europe.

Customers would learn that the 777 economy class would use 18.5-inch seats, more than an inch wider than those specified for the Airbus jetliners. Also, there would be 10.75 inches of head clearance aboard the 777, compared to 5.22 inches in an A340. It is always easier to market a jetliner with more headroom. (Legroom is another matter, and plane makers leave that up to the airlines by providing movable seats.)

Boeing's only remaining global competitor, Airbus Industrie, was expanding its line to include its largest aircraft to date. The A330 and A340 would face off against the 777 and would be suggested as an alternative for users of the 747-400 who often had to serve routes with less than full loads, and who might want something smaller than a 747-400 but larger than a 767.

As noted earlier, Boeing had faced stiff competition from Airbus since the early days of the 757 and 767 programs. Many at Boeing saw this as an unfair competition because Airbus Industrie, a multinational consortium of European aerospace companies, is subsidized by the governments of France, Germany, Spain, and the United Kingdom. As such, it has a financial safety net to protect it from potential downturns in the jetliner market.

Boeing, of course, is a private company with no government subsidy for new jetliner projects. The fact that they were competing against a government-subsidized entity was not lost on the people who were working on the 777, an aircraft that they hoped would ultimately be more popular with airlines and passengers than the Airbus aircraft.

### Three Companies, Three Engines, and Three Assumptions

Since the beginning of the history of aviation, the single most complex—and generally the most expensive—part of any aircraft program has been the engine or engines. Beginning with the jumbo jet era in the early 1990s, it had become customary for aircraft manufacturers to offer customers a choice of engines. This made good marketing sense and provided good customer service, but it also added to the complexity of the design process. By the time the 777 went onto the CATIA drawing boards at Everett in 1989, it was already assumed that Boeing would offer an engine choice.

The firms in the forefront of engine development since the beginning of the jet age are Pratt & Whitney in Connecticut, General Electric in Ohio, and Britain's Rolls-Royce. A fourth company, CFM International, is a consortium that brings together General Electric with the French company, SNECMA (Société National d'Etudes et Construction de Moteurs d'Avion), to produce the CFM56 series of high-bypass turbofan engines. Of course, this slate of jet engine manufacturers also supplies engines to the multinational Airbus Industrie.

The process that would lead to three engine *types* that would ultimately be specified for the 777 program began with three assumptions.

First, these engines would be high-bypass turbofan engines—the larger, more powerful, and more efficient genre of engines that began to replace turbojet engines at the beginning of the jumbo jet era. In addition to their desirability from a fuel-efficiency standpoint, turbofans are cleaner and quieter, to meet increasingly restrictive standards mandated by the American Federal Aviation Administration (FAA), the European Joint Aviation Authority (JAA), and other agencies.

FAR RIGHT
This breathtaking view of a 777 winging its way west at sunrise was created through the use of computer technology for release to Boeing customers and other interested parties at the Paris Air Show in June 1991. In 1995, Paris Air Show attendees would be traveling to France aboard real 777 aircraft.

This beautifully lit photograph of Boeing's 1/40th scale model of the 777 was used by Boeing in the early 1990s to underscore the fact that the aircraft's 60-foot 6-inch all-composite tail was the largest ever used on a twin-jet.

Second, the new engines would not be off-the-shelf models. They would be the largest jet engines ever manufactured by these companies for a commercial jetliner.

Third was the assumption that the 777 would be a twin-engine aircraft. In the beginning of the design process, designers considered a four-engine 777 with smaller off-the-shelf engines. Because the airframe would have a gross weight 60 percent greater than that of the 767, clearly it would need more power than the two engines that powered the 767. However, a decision was made to make the 777 a twin-engine aircraft. Two engines would simplify both manufacturing and maintenance of the aircraft, and by 1989 the technology existed to permit the manufacturing of such engines.

Another factor in the decision to go with two engines rather than four was changing regulations regarding Extended-range Twin-engine Operations (ETOPS). In the early days of commercial jet transportation in the 1950s and 1960s, turbojet engines were not nearly as reliable as more recent jet engines. Multiple engines were considered to be a safety factor, especially in long over-water flights. The loss of one of two engines over an ocean would be disastrous if the remaining engine was not adequate to fly and land the aircraft. Indeed, Boeing's own 727 was designed during the 1960s as a tri-jet rather than as a twin-jet to satisfy safety requirements.

In this February 1992 photograph, Boeing engineers Dave Kirkland and Tom Wong posed with the recently completed 40th-scale fiberglass model of the 777. While useful in the engineering and design phase of the 777 program, such models had been made virtually unnecessary by computer modeling. The 19-pound model took more than 250 hours to build.

# WHO IS AIRBUS INDUSTRIE?

The four principal partners within the Airbus Industrie consortium are Aerospatiale in France, DaimlerChrysler Aerospace (formerly Deutsche Aerospace) in Germany, British Aerospace in the United Kingdom, and Spain's CASA (Construcciones Aeronauticas, Sociedad Anónima). Aircraft parts and components are manufactured in each of these countries, and final assembly of Airbus aircraft takes place in Toulouse, France. The governments of all four nations subsidize Airbus Industrie to cushion it from market fluctuations.

As the power and reliability of newer-technology turbofan engines increased dramatically, regulations changed as well, and ETOPS was first authorized in 1985. An aircraft could operate more than two hours flight time from land with two engines, but each of the engines would have to be powerful enough to get the aircraft to an airport safely. Within the industry, the acronym ETOPS was still often translated half-jokingly as "Engines Turn On or Passengers Swim." Various aircraft—including Boeing's 757, 767, and later 737s—had been granted ETOPS approval

In October 1990, United Airlines became the Boeing's first customer for the 777. Obviously, orders for new aircraft predate delivery by many months, so it is typical for aircraft manufacturers to produce artist's renderings of aircraft in a new customer's livery for release to the media before the first actual aircraft is ready. This January 1992 illustration shows a 777 in United Airlines livery, but it is of special historic interest because it depicts a color scheme that the airline would phase out before the delivery of the first 777 in 1995.

some time after they entered service, but with the 777, Boeing intended to design in an inherent ETOPS capability.

The three engines were being designed at the same time that the 777 itself was taking shape on the CATIA screens at Everett and across the globe. They would include Pratt & Whitney's PW4000 series, General Electric's all-new GE90 series, and the Rolls-Royce Trent 800 series. It was decided that Pratt & Whitney engines would be used on the first several aircraft and the other engines would enter the flight-test program in stages as it unfolded.

The three engine families would be much larger in both size and power than the families of engines offered for aircraft in the 767 class, with larger-diameter fans and bypass ratios ranging from 6-to-1 to as high as 9-to-1, compared to the 5-to-1 ratio for engines used on 747s. Thrust ratings would range from 74,000 to 77,000 pounds, roughly 60 percent greater than the rating of the engine class that first equipped the 767. Surprisingly, the new and more powerful engines developed for the 777 would actually prove to be quieter than those used in the 767.

# BUILDING A GIANT JETLINER

As breathtaking and groundbreaking as it was for its time, the digital design procedure embodied in CATIA represented less than a quarter of the total process of designing, fabricating, and testing the 777. By the summer of 1992, the CATIA crews had done their work, and pieces of actual 777 hardware began appearing across the Puget Sound area.

At Renton, you could walk through the cabin mockup, while across the street from Boeing Field in Seattle, work was being completed on the Boeing Commercial Airplane Group Integrated Aircraft Systems Laboratory (IASL). This facility was intended to bring together in a single site more than two dozen separate laboratories involved in more than a hundred aspects of commercial aircraft development. Much of the hardware testing and simulation for the 777—and later aircraft as well—would be carried out under IASL's one-half-million-square-foot roof.

## Cutting Metal

In July 1992 workers began laying out an "Iron Bird" test rig at the IASL. The purpose was to study the 777's fly-by-wire control system in real time. Cables, wiring, and actuators were laid out on the floor of the IASL in the approximate spatial relationship of their counterparts in the real 777. By the spring of 1993, Iron Bird tests were in progress.

Just as CATIA had revolutionized the design process for the 777, it strongly affected the work being done at the IASL and in the subsequent manufacturing process. A by-product of the CATIA design process was a virtual library of digitally defined components. Such "libraries" had existed previously within the company, but they had been compartmentalized, and cross-referencing was a cumbersome process.

During the mating process of Section 41 and Section 43 of the *777* fuselage, the forward section is hoisted up on the big 40-ton crane at the Boeing Commercial Airplane Group Everett factory. As indicated in this February 1995 photograph, this was the first *777-200* for Hong Kong's Cathay Pacific. It was also the first aircraft of the series to be certified with the Rolls-Royce Trent engine option.

In July 1992 crews at Boeing's Integrated Aircraft Systems Laboratory (IASL) in Seattle began laying out an "Iron Bird" test rig to study the 777 control system. To test this "fly-by-wire" system, IASL used pulleys, cables, and hundreds of electrical wires to simulate the system. Such tests began in the spring of 1993. The blue steel structure seen here was the foundation for the Iron Bird's moving wing surfaces, including spoilers and flaperons.

Now, with an aircraft that was 100 percent designed with CATIA, the manufacturing people would be able to access all of the digital data and adapt it to actually building the aircraft. The computer system that would facilitate this next key step is known as Define & Control Airplane Configuration/Manufacturing Resource Management (DCAC/MRM). This mouthful of alphabet soup would allow the folks at Everett to digitally manage the entire production process.

Like CATIA, the DCAC/MRM system used computers to bring digital efficiency into what had been an analog world. The DCAC/MRM system also allowed Boeing to better work with—and coordinate the work of—its archipelago of suppliers and subcontractors, and do this more efficiently than before. Tens of thousands of employees could now access a single source of product data throughout the manufacturing process. Eventually, the DCAC/MRM system would grow to encompass all of the Boeing Commercial Airplane Group programs. The combination of CATIA with the DCAC/MRM system is estimated to have saved about a third in the time and cost of building 777 airframes. This would also prove to be an enormous boon to Boeing's spare parts business.

During the late winter of 1993, the virtual aircraft was starting to evolve as a concrete—actually aluminum—first 777. In Everett, metal had been cut and was being formed into struts and stringers. In the Kansas heartland, Boeing crews at the Wichita Division were assembling the first engine struts and wheelwells.

By now, responsibility for various major subsystems had been parcelled out. Everett, of course, would be the final assembly site, and would manufacture various major structural subsystems. Indeed, by October, Boeing would complete its project to increase floor space at Everett by 50 percent.

Meanwhile, Wichita had been delegated the design and manufacturing responsibilities for the struts and nacelles for all three of the engine series specified for the 777. Subassemblies for wing spars were to be manufactured at the newly established Boeing Tacoma skin and spar manufacturing plant, a two- or three- hour drive south of Everett.

## Come Together

After four years of design work that overlapped about two years of hardware and tooling preparation, the major assembly of

A machinist at the Boeing Commercial Airplane Group skin and spar factory in Tacoma inspects the raw material that will be milled to produce a lower-wing skin panel for a 777 aircraft. The material would be lowered onto a specially designed, 270-foot Cincinnati Millicron skin mill, one of the largest in the world. This 950,000-square-foot manufacturing plant at Tacoma began work on 777 program-related assemblies in July 1992.

the first 777 wing spar and nose sections officially got underway on January 21, 1993. The first immediately recognizable segment of the 777 to take shape at Everett was a test version of Section 41, the nose section. It was constructed as final verification that parts designed and "preassembled" in virtual space would fit. They did.

By using digital preassembly of computer-generated three-dimensional solid images, proper fit was ensured. Design engineers and manufacturing engineers worked on the design of the same parts simultaneously, and this would have the effect of decreasing subsequent change orders. In turn, this would increase efficiency in building and installing the actual parts at the manufacturing stages. It was here that cost savings began to mount.

This worker at the Boeing Commercial Airplane Group's Wichita Division is preparing a stretch-form block for skin-stretching a panel for a 777 aircraft. Pulled on the L-1000 stretch press under 550 tons of pressure, this skin section measures 94 by 460 inches (over half the length of a bowling alley) and was the largest stretched at the Wichita plant.

Employees at the Wichita Division of the Boeing Commercial Airplane Group assemble the lower spar for the strut that would support one of the two engines of a 777—in this case, a Pratt & Whitney PW4084 engine, one of several choices offered by Boeing to 777 customers. The Wichita facility had design and manufacturing responsibilities for the struts and nacelles for all the 777 engine types.

Throughout 1993, parts and components streamed into Everett from throughout the United States, and in May the first major fuselage sections for the 777 began to arrive from the Japanese Aircraft Development Corporation (JADC). The countdown to the first flight of the first 777 aircraft was on everyone's mind at the Boeing Commercial Airplane Group, but the parts were coming in not simply for that airframe and that event, but to stock the shelves for the ongoing production program that would immediately follow the completion of the prototype.

The first major "body join" saw the mating of Section 41 and Section 43 of the 777, the two forward fuselage sections of airframe number one. The wings were joined next, and then the tail surfaces. On December 15, the "final body join" brought together the definitive parts to make the first 777 look like an airplane.

Just as CATIA saved time and money when making changes in the design process, the digitization of manufacturing would

allow great savings in customizing the production aircraft. Only rarely are individual jetliners identical. Airline customers express preferences for everything from the color of the carpeting and the location of the lavatories, to the exact configuration of flight decks. Each of these variations traditionally requires engineering drawings, which take time and cost money. Some variations can be anticipated, but others cannot. Regardless, they are always more time-consuming in the analog world than they are when a digital model already exists.

Changes involved in customizing aircraft can be extremely complex—especially when millions of parts are potentially involved. Of course, the parts themselves are only a portion of the equation. The interfaces and relationships, especially spatial relationships, between the parts are especially critical. If the size or shape of a part changes, then so must the parts next to it, and possibly the parts next to those. For example, specific wheels require specific tires and specific brakes, and different engines require specific interfaces that extend throughout the entire airframe. Indeed, more than 10,000 individual interfaces were in the 777 digital mockup, many with tolerances in the range of .01 inch. Some of them were so tiny that they were of a nature that

The room was in near darkness, then the music began and the lights began to come on. The lighting was barely perceptible at first, and then suddenly, there she was! Dramatic lighting, complete with lasers and projections of customer logos, added to the dramatic atmosphere that accompanied the rollout of the first 777 on April 9, 1994.

might not have been discovered until final assembly had traditional pencil-on-Mylar drawings been used.

It has been said that CATIA allowed Boeing to exceed its goal of reducing changes and reworking by 50 percent. Indeed, in some instances, rework was estimated to have been reduced by 90 percent. Laser alignment tool readings showed one wing perfect and the other just .002 inch out of alignment. Over the length of the aircraft, a distance of just over 209 feet, the fuselage was off by only .003 to .008 inch horizontally. Overall, the components fitted together better than anticipated and at the highest level of quality. The first 777 was an average of .023 inch—about the thickness of a business card—from perfect alignment in all directions. Boeing has observed that most airplanes line up to within a half inch. The 777 was better than a quarter of a tenth of an inch.

## Rollout

There is something in human nature that craves a celebration to mark the completion of intense and extraordinary tasks. In the aircraft industry, such celebrations occur at the auspicious moment of the completion of the first airframe in what is hoped will be a long and successful production run. These celebrations are called "rollouts." They are the symbolic rolling through the factory door of the new aircraft, although in many cases the aircraft has been rolled into its place of honor before the partygoers arrive, and it often remains stationary throughout the festivities.

The guest list for a rollout starts with the workers who have built the new aircraft, and who will build her sister ships. It is a moment of accomplishment for them. Executives of the airframe manufacturer, the subcontractors, and the engine-makers are also on hand, and it is a proud moment for them as well.

If there are *guests of honor*—other than the aircraft itself, usually referred to familiarly as "herself"—they are the representatives of the customers, for they are the ones who have paid for all of this. In the case of a commercial rollout, the logos of all the airline customers who

The first 777 actually rolled out the big doors of the Boeing Everett plant five days after the official rollout. Although there was no fanfare and no crowd this time, the interest of those present was just as intense. The big aircraft was then taken to the Everett flight line for fuel systems installation and other preparations for the first flight, which would occur eight weeks later.

have placed preproduction advance orders are painted (or applied as decals) on the forward fuselage of the aircraft. This warms the hearts of even the most business-like of airline corporate executives.

For the 777 program, the big day came on April 9, 1994. The scene was the sprawling Boeing Commercial Airplane Group factory complex at Everett, and it was estimated that 100,000 people were on hand. The scene was quite theatrical, complete with dramatic lighting and suspenseful music. Indeed, there have been some rollouts—such as that of the Northrop B-2 in 1988—for which original orchestral music was composed.

The 777 herself was initially just a curtained silhouette in the darkness as projectors flashed customer and supplier logos through the gloom. At last, though, the lights came up and "she" made her official debut.

Captain John Cashman (left), designated as 777 chief pilot, and his boss, Captain Ken Higgins, the director of the Boeing Commercial Airplane Group Flight Test organization, served as the flight crew for the debut flight of the 777 on June 12, 1994. Between them, they represented 60 years of flying experience. Cashman would later be named as Chief Pilot of the Boeing Commercial Airplane Group.

Aircraft Number One was painted in the red, white, and blue Boeing livery. The fuselage carried the logos of United Airlines, the launch customer, as well as the other airlines who had consulted closely with Boeing during the development process, such as British Airways and Hong Kong's Cathay Pacific.

Japan had been an integral part of the process, and the logos also included All Nippon Airways, Japan Air System, and Japan Airlines. Other airlines who earned an honored spot on the fuselage by placing orders before the rollout included Korean Air, Asiana, Continental Airlines, Thai Airways International (THAI), and Emirates, the flag carrier of the United Arab Emirates.

To summarize the special thread of collaborative effort involving airlines and Japanese industrial partners that had run through the entire 777 program, the slogan "Working Together" was painted in red logotype script beneath the flight deck window ahead of the forward fuselage doors.

The rollout ceremony behind her, the first 777 actually rolled out the big doors of the Boeing Everett plant five days later with no fanfare and just a small crowd, comprised mainly of Boeing employees. She had been painted for the April 9 show, and her engines had been hung. She looked like a finished airplane, but there was still work left to do.

## First Flight

Often less dramatic than a rollout, but far more important, is the first flight of a new aircraft type. A great deal of experience and engineering goes into such a machine, and theoretically there should be no doubt of a first flight's success. However, seldom does such a day dawn that one does not hear the whispered "Will she fly?"

In the early days of aviation, there were many occasions when she didn't. As aircraft have gotten stratospherically more expensive to design and build, care is taken to troubleshoot every possible reason why the airplane might *not* fly. But even today, nobody really knows for sure until the wheels come up.

With the 777, the first flight was especially significant. She was not just any new aircraft but the first all-digital jetliner, and she would be a true technological pioneer. Like no airplane before, the 777 had been designed entirely by computer. It had been proven that such an aircraft could be designed and assembled, but would she fly?

The misty morning of June 12, 1994, held the answer. The first 777 was on the tarmac at Everett wearing the suitable registration number N7771. The flight crew would consist of two veteran Boeing test pilots. Captain John Cashman, whom the Commercial Airplane Group had named chief pilot for the 777 flight-test program, would be flying in the right seat as first officer, or copilot. In the pilot's seat would be Cashman's boss, Captain Ken Higgins, who was the director of the entire Boeing Commercial Airplane Group Flight Test organization. As Boeing noted in a contemporary press release, they represented, between them, 60 years of flying experience. Both also had many hours in the Boeing Commercial Airplane Group 777 flight simulator and were as familiar with the big aircraft's flight deck as anyone could be.

**ABOVE**
Applying takeoff power to the two Pratt & Whitney PW4084 high-bypass turbofan engines, John Cashman and Ken Higgins deftly lift N7771, marking the first take-off in the 777 flight test program.

**LEFT**
The first 777 (appropriately serialed N7771) taxis past a corner of the Boeing Commercial Airplane Group facility at Everett in preparation for its first flight from Paine Field on June 12, 1994. The weather was typical for June in western Washington—mild with patchy clouds. Whidbey Island is visible in Puget Sound in the distance.

After a walk-around and an extensive preflight check, Cashman and Higgins powered up the two big Pratt & Whitney PW4084 turbofans. They taxied N7771 out to adjacent Paine Field and aligned the big aircraft with Runway 34 Left. At 11:43 A.M., with tower clearance, the debut flight was deemed good to go.

The flight crew throttled up to takeoff power, and at 11:45 officially, N7771 was airborne.

71

# THE 777 PROGRAM:
# THE FIRST 30 AIRCRAFT OFF THE LINE

| Registration | First Customer Delivery | Engine |
|---|---|---|
| 1. N7771 (later B-HNL) | Cathay Pacific (December 6, 2000) | PW4084 (later Trent 884) |
| 2. N7772 (later N774UA) | United Airlines (March, 29 1996) | PW4077 |
| 3. N7773 (later N7771UA) | United Airlines (November 27, 1995) | PW4077 |
| 4. N7774 (later N773UA) | United Airlines (January 31, 1996) | PW4077 |
| 5. N772UA | United Airlines (September 29, 1995) | PW4077 |
| 6. N77779 (later G-ZZZA) | British Airways (May 20, 1996) | GE90-76B |
| 7. N777UA | United Airlines (May 15, 1995) | PW4077 |
| 8. N77776 (later N766UA) | United Airlines (May 24, 1995) | PW4077 |
| 9. N77774 (later N767UA) | United Airlines (May 31, 1995) | PW4077 |
| 10. N77771 (later G-ZZZB) | British Airways (March 28, 1997) | GE90-76B |
| 11. N77775 (later N768UA) | United Airlines (June 26, 1995) | PW4077 |
| 12. N77773 (later N769UA) | United Airlines (June 28, 1995) | PW4077 |
| 13. N77772 (later N770UA) | United Airlines (July 13, 1995) | PW4077 |
| 14. N77772 (later VR-HNA, B-HNA) | Cathay Pacific (August 23, 1996) | Trent 877 |
| 15. N5014K (later G-ZZZC) | British Airways (November 11, 1995) | GE90-76B |
| 16. N5016R (later JA8197) | All Nippon Airways (October 4, 1995) | PW4074 |
| 17. G-ZZZD | British Airways (December 28, 1995) | GE90-76B |
| 18. N77773 (later VR-HNB, B-HNB) | Cathay Pacific (October 25, 1996) | Trent 877 |
| 19. G-ZZZE | British Airways (January 12, 1996) | GE90-76B |
| 20. B2051 | China Southern Airlines (December 28, 1995) | GE90-85B |
| 21. JA8198 | All Nippon Airways (December 21, 1995) | PW4074 |
| 22. N775UA | United Airlines (January 22, 1996) | PW4077 |
| 23. JA8981 | Japan Airlines (February 15, 1996) | PW4084 |
| 24. N5017V (later B2052) | China Southern Airlines (February 28, 1996) | GE90-85B |
| 25. HS-TJA | Thai Airways International (March 31, 1996) | Trent 875 |
| 26. JA8982 | Japan Airlines (March 28, 1996) | PW4084 |
| 27. N776UA | United Airlines (April 11, 1996) | PW4077 |
| 28. VR-HNC (later B-HNC) | Cathay Pacific (May 9, 1996) | Trent 877 |
| 29. JA8199 | All Nippon Airways (May 23, 1996) | PW4074 |
| 30. A6-EMD | Emirates (June 5, 1996) | Trent 871 |

The first 777, registered as N7771, paces a T-38 chase plane over the green hills of western Washington during her maiden flight on June 12, 1994. Flight crew John Cashman and Ken Higgins conducted what was described by Boeing as a near-flawless flight before returning to touch down at Paine Field three hours and 48 minutes after they took off.

The first flight took N7771 out across Puget Sound, and eventually up to a maximum altitude of 19,000 feet. Cashman and Higgins worked through the entire first flight checklist, including shutting down and restarting one of the PW4084s. Three hours and 48 minutes after they had retracted the landing gear, they had N7771 back on the ground at Paine Field. The flight-test program, which would last for 11 months and eventually involve nine aircraft, had begun.

## Flight Testing

Flight testing is the penultimate step in the process of building a jetliner. Certification is always the final step in the flight-test process, and it is the ultimate goal of the flight-test program.

In April 1995, less than a year after the first flight, the 777 would receive its type certification simultaneously from the FAA and the European JAA. But that is getting ahead of the story. There would be a great deal of work squeezed into those ten months.

Typically, although not always, the first aircraft of a series to roll out is literally a series prototype. It is earmarked only for flight-testing, and destined never to carry passengers or serve a customer. For instance, Boeing's prototype 707, 727, 747, and 767 remained company-owned and marked in Boeing livery for many years. The 707 prototype was donated to the Smithsonian Institution's National Air & Space Museum and was flown there for exhibit at Washington Dulles Airport after four decades of *not* flying commercial airline routes. This writer last saw the first 747 parked at Boeing Field in Seattle more than three decades after its debut.

From an economic standpoint, however, it makes more sense to put every airframe to work, and such would be the case with the 777 program. Although United Airlines was the launch customer for the 777 program, the first 777, N7771, would not go to United Airlines after flight testing. In December 2000, five years after her flight-test sister ships had already gone into airline service, N7771 was delivered to Cathay Pacific and re-registered as B-HNL. She was also re-engined with Rolls-Royce high-bypass turbofan engines (see sidebar).

In the four months following N7771's maiden flight, an additional three 777s rolled out at Everett. By October 1994, the 777 roll-outs had become routine—no music, no dramatic lighting. Unlike N7771, which would fly for half a decade in Boeing livery, the next four ships were all delivered in United

Registered as N7771, the first 777 banks toward home over the snowcapped peaks of the Olympic Range west of Puget Sound. Mount Rainier, Washington's highest peak, can be seen in the distance. Including N7771, there were nine 777-200 aircraft involved in the Boeing test program. All of them eventually were delivered to airline customers, most to United Airlines. However, Cathay Pacific took delivery of N7771 in 2000 and re-registered it as B-HNL.

Airlines paint, the same paint that they would wear when they actually went to work. However, they carried interim registration numbers, and would be re-registered when United took them over (see sidebar).

Ultimately, there would be nine 777s in the flight-test program, although they were not all among the first nine to be built. Seven of the first ten aircraft built *were* flight-test aircraft, but the ninth flight-test 777 would actually be the 18th off the assembly line.

The fourth aircraft, registered as N7774, made its first flight on October 28, 1994. It was notable in that it was designated to be used in a series of 1,000 flight cycles, the equivalent of a year's worth of daily service. This line of testing was undertaken by

In October 1994, 777 aircraft number N7771 was flown down to Edwards Air Force Base for testing. Seen here is the Velocity Minimum Unstick (VMU) test designed to determine the slowest speed at which the aircraft can take off. A laser distance and speed meter (LD90-3100-GF) with a MK42-Z80 glass-fiber coupled optical head was mounted on the aircraft's tail, looking downward. A laminated oak skid protected the tail from damage.

Boeing and United Airlines as a supplement to standard certification flight tests. The idea was to demonstrate 777 reliability in simulated heavy-use airline operating environments, and its readiness for long-distance routes.

N7774 was powered by the Pratt & Whitney engines, but it would soon be joined by other aircraft that would fly 1,000 flight cycles on General Electric and Rolls-Royce engines. During the latter nine percent of this 1,000-cycle validation program, totaling about 400 hours, Boeing crews would be joined by United Airlines ground and flight personnel.

The first flight with an engine other than the Pratt & Whitney came on February 2, 1995, with Chief Pilot John

During flight tests in 1994, the cabin interior of the prototype 777 was filled with what at first glance looked like aluminum beer kegs. In fact, these 55-gallon barrels contained water. The contents of two dozen barrels in the forward cabin and a like number of barrels in the aft section were pumped back and forth to simulate shifts in center of gravity that would result from passengers moving about. The top photo shows the cabin as it is when the 777 is delivered.

Cashman and Project Pilot Captain Frank Santoni at the controls. The five-hour, 20-minute flight featured the sixth 777. It was temporarily registered in the United States as N77779, but already painted in the livery of British Airways, to whom she would eventually be delivered. The engine was not, however, the British-made Rolls-Royce Trent, but rather the second American engine, the General Electric GE90. After two years in the flight-test program, N7779 would be turned over to British Airways in March 1997 and re-registered as G-ZZZB.

The first flight test of a 777 with the Trent 877 series engine came on May 26, 1995. It was the 14th airframe and the eighth 777 earmarked for the flight-test program. Temporarily registered as N77772, the aircraft would be delivered to Cathay Pacific in August 1996 and re-registered as VR-HNA. In 1997, when Hong Kong was returned to China, the aircraft was re-registered again, with the Chinese "B" prefix, as B-HNA.

## Time For ETOPS

Although testing would continue for more than a year, on April 19, 1995, the 777 was formally certified, receiving its type-design certification from both the United States FAA and the European JAA. This marked the first time that a commercial aircraft had received its certification from both regulatory agencies on the same day. Also in the package was FAA production certification that authorized Boeing to put the aircraft into production.

By May 22, the 777 test fleet had accumulated a combined total of 1,950 flights and 3,664 hours of flight time. Yet one final regulatory hurdle still remained—the need to obtain official approval for Extended-range Twin-engine Operations (ETOPS). Boeing had designed the 777 from the beginning to be ETOPS-capable, but just as there were those who whispered, "Will she fly?" there were those who joked that ETOPS really meant "Engines Turn On or Passengers Swim."

However, ETOPS was no laughing matter. Customers did not simply expect ETOPS capability, they insisted on it.

During the flight-test cycle, a 777 with Pratt & Whitney engines had been tested and flown under all appropriate conditions to prove it is capable of flying up to 180-minute ETOPS missions. During flight testing, the 777 would perform eight 180-minute single-engine diversions for a total of 24 hours. This would be the equivalent of all the diversion hours accumulated by the entire Boeing 767 fleet during the initial five years of its ETOPS operations.

Although all previous aircraft had received their green light for ETOPS *after* they had been in service awhile, it was now theoretically possible to obtain this certification "out of the box." Boeing's customers wanted to open their boxes and find an ETOPS-certified 777. Boeing had planned ahead in order to make this happen, and it was time to deliver. The first

The third 777 to be built, this aircraft was also the first 777 to visit Europe. In November 1994, with a 70-person crew aboard, it was flown to Sondre Stromfjord in Greenland for cold-weather tests. When the weather proved to be "unseasonably warm," the aircraft had to be flown to Kiruna in northern Sweden, as seen here, where temperatures were a crisp minus seven Fahrenheit.

aircraft was already scheduled to start carrying passengers for United Airlines in June, two months after the original FAA/JAA certification.

On April 30, 1995, in order to underscore the ETOPS capability, a flight-test 777 returning from a three-week world-wide publicity tour flew 7,850 miles nonstop—and over water—from Bangkok, Thailand, to Seattle. In making the flight in 13 hours and 36 minutes, the aircraft established a new speed record for the route.

On May 30, 1995, the 777 became the first aircraft in aviation history to earn FAA ETOPS approval *before* it entered service. In a ceremony held at Boeing Field, Ron Wagner, the manager of the FAA's Aircraft Certification Service Transport Airplane Directorate, formally presented the ETOPS approval. Dave Hegy, manager of the FAA Certification Management Office was also on hand to announce that United Airlines had successfully complied with the requirements of their ETOPS plan and had demonstrated the ability to operate and maintain the 777 in a manner consistent with that required for 180-minute ETOPS operations. For his part, Ron Woodard, the president of the Boeing Commercial Airplane Group, added that the aircraft had "finished one of the most thorough laboratory, ground, and flight-testing efforts in aviation history."

The way was now clear for the aircraft to go into service.

# PAINTING THE 777

BELOW
*Finishing touches are applied to a Thai Airways International (THAI) 777-2DT at the Boeing Commercial Airplane Group paint hangar in Everett. Boeing understands that the use of exterior decorative paint on its aircraft is very important to its customers, because it projects their corporate image and differentiates them from other operators. As a result, overall appearance is as important a requirement of any exterior paint as its durability.*

*A Saudi Arabian Airlines 777-268 is made ready to be pulled from the Boeing Commercial Airplane Group paint hangar at Everett. Typically, Boeing jetliners receive a three-step finish: the conversion coating, the primer, and finally, after the primer cures, three spray passes of topcoat to achieve a coating 3 to 5 mils thick. The taping, painting, and curing process may be repeated several times to finish a particular paint scheme.*

*A Kuwait Airways 777-269ER emerges from the Boeing Commercial Airplane Group paint hangar in Everett. In 1998, Boeing made the changes to improve the color and gloss durability of topcoat paint and meet new regulations that mandated the use of primers and topcoats with low volatile organic compound content.*

BELOW

*The Japan Airlines 777-346, Regulus, in the Boeing Commercial Airplane Group paint hangar at Everett. Boeing's electrostatic paint guns emit larger paint droplets that lose less solvent during spraying than do other types of paint guns. Because of this, the paint flows more easily and produces a smoother finish.*

At first glance, these wheelwell frames being inserted into rivet assembly jigs look like fuselage sections with flight deck windows. At Boeing's Wichita facility, work was done on freestanding jigs such as these, which are mounted on sliding frames so that they can be stowed off the factory floor when not in use to save space. Digitally designed and built, these machine tools range in size up to 217 inches and are used for the *777* nose section.

ABOVE
Seen here in June 1993 at work on stringers for the first 777 wing is one of Boeing's then-new automated fastening machines. Located at the 777 Division facility near Everett, this machine was the first of its kind to install rivets, as well as nuts and threaded fasteners (bolts and screws). It precisely gauges each hole before the rivets are inserted. Inserting more than 28 types of fasteners at a rate of six per minute, the machine would be capable of completing a wing in three days.

RIGHT
A 777 wing spar is seen here in a giant automated assembly tool at the Boeing Commercial Airplane Group factory in Everett. Subassemblies for the huge wing spars come to Everett from various locations, including the Boeing Tacoma skin and spar manufacturing plant.

A wheelwell for a 777 takes shape at the Boeing Wichita facility. Made of titanium and aluminum, the parts are assembled using statistical control process techniques to ensure minimum variability of hardware, consistent quality, and proper fit. The shiny steel component in the center is part of the nose wheel strut's axle assembly.

Seen here at the Boeing Commercial Airplane Group Developmental Center in Seattle is a developmental version of the 777 horizontal stabilizer being tested. In April 1993 the hydraulic jacks at the bottom pulled the tips of this 44-foot component down until it was stressed beyond the "ultimate load," or 150 percent greater than the greatest stress expected to be encountered in airline operations.

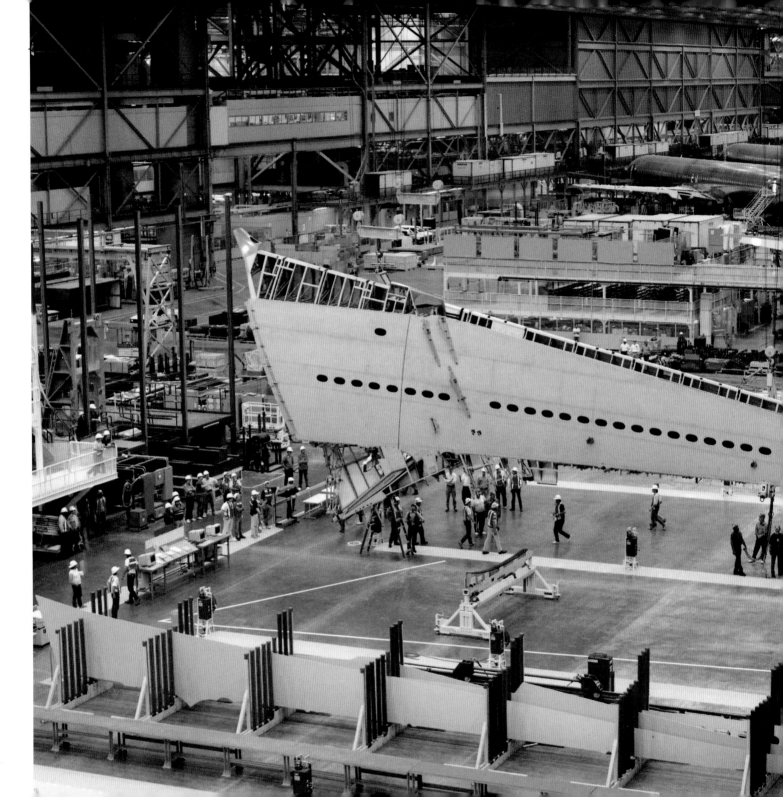

ABOVE

A completed left wing for the 777 is hoisted out of its production tool by means of two gigantic high-technology cranes. The blue "wheel" is a turning fixture that is used for rotating 777 fuselage sections. The 14-ton wing is about to be tested to make sure that its integral fuel tank is fuel-tight. Then it will be painted and moved to its next assembly position for the installation of ductwork and tubing for hydraulics and fuel.

A 14-ton 777 left wing section "flies" through the Boeing Commercial Airplane Group Everett factory. The 90-foot section has just been completed and is being hoisted out of its production tool to be repositioned onto the white cradle, where internal and external work will be done. In the background, a group of smaller 767 aircraft are in final assembly.

85

The major structural components of the 777 begin to come together on the floor at Everett when the completed set of wing sections are joined to the center fuselage section. The resulting structure, weighing 45 tons, will then move to the next position on the assembly line for curing the seal of the wing-to-body area.

RIGHT
The 45-ton wing-to-body section of the first 777 is brought in to be mated to Section 41 (the nose section) at the Boeing Commercial Airplane Group Everett facility. Platforms to allow workers access to the big swept wings are already in place. Most of the remaining assembly steps will occur with the aircraft in this position.

With the wing-to-body middle section of the 777 aligned with the nose section, the big 40-ton crane delivers the aft fuselage section into the mix. Additional structural components will be delivered to this location as needed. With all of the platforms in place, the full structural assembly will happen on this spot. When the 777 leaves, it will appear complete.

As the 777 fuselage sections are mated, they appear to be swallowed by the catwalks that allow workers access to every necessary point on the big ship. Then the tail arrives for attachment. The rudder always arrives pre-painted, so that when it is balanced, it will weigh exactly the same as when the aircraft is first flown.

A 777 Fuselage Section 43, with the wings attached, is brought into position to be mated with the aft fuselage section at the Boeing Everett facility. The doors are being installed in the aft section, and the windows—covered by heavy layers of protective plastic—are already in.

LEFT
To build a proper series of aircraft, it is necessary to destroy one. Although CATIA simulated the stress loads on the 777 structure, the second 777 aircraft to be built was systematically torn apart to test it under stress. Computer-controlled hydraulic actuators applied approximately 500,000 pounds of pressure to each wing to simulate 150 percent of the maximum pressure likely to be experienced by a 777 under the most extreme flight conditions. Moments after this picture was taken, the right wing broke—at exactly the point where CATIA had predicted that it would.

RIGHT
The sixth Boeing 777 built for British Airways was also the first Increased Gross Weight 777 built for the flag carrier of the United Kingdom. Originally given the "IGW" designation, these aircraft became operational as the 777-200ER "Extended Range" series.

# THE 777 GOES TO WORK

The 777 would be one of the biggest aviation news items for 1995. It was the kind of publicity that marketing people like to hear and repeat, and which engineering types like to think of as a pat on the back. First to receive honors would be the people who had been part of the nearly 300 teams who had worked the long hours at those CATIA workstations. On June 14, 1995, a year after the first flight, the 777 program received a Smithsonian Computerworld Award for "digital product definition and preassembly in manufacturing."

At the end of the year, the 777 program would receive aviation's highest accolade: the Robert J. Collier Trophy, awarded to the top aeronautical achievement of the year. The National Aeronautic Association officially awarded the trophy at ceremonies on February 15, 1996. Also during 1996, the aircraft would be awarded the 1996 Trophy for Current Achievement by the Smithsonian Institution's National Air & Space Museum.

But the 777 had not been designed as a museum piece. For the 777 herself, the truly big news of 1995 was that she was finally on the job.

## The Launch Customer Launches Service

On May 15, 1995, Boeing formally made the first airline delivery of a 777 to launch customer United Airlines in a ceremony at Seattle's Museum of Flight at Boeing Field. As had been the case at the rollout 13 months earlier, the "Working Together" logo was very much in evidence. Registered with the apropos designation N777UA, this aircraft was the seventh 777 off the assembly line and the third 777 to be built that was not originally part of the flight-test fleet.

The second 777 series ever built is seen here framed against Mount Rainier, Washington state's signature natural landmark and a favorite backdrop for Boeing photographers for nearly a century. Originally, it was registered by Boeing as N77772, but it was delivered to United Airlines as a 777-222 under the registration N774UA.

The 50th 777 series aircraft to be delivered was the 57th aircraft on the line. Boeing's launch customer for the 777 series, United Airlines, took delivery of this milestone aircraft, N782UA, on March 7, 1997. It had been nine months since the delivery of the first 777. The 100th would be delivered just seven months after the 50th.

On May 24 and 31, during the week that ETOPS certification was granted, United Airlines received its second and third 777s. Registered as N766UA and N767UA, they had been the eighth and ninth aircraft off the line and were registered as N77776 and N77774 during the flight-test program. Two more deliveries would follow in June.

Three weeks after the first delivery, on June 7, United Airlines put its new fleet to work with three virtually simultaneous inaugural flights. The first departure was N777UA, flying as Flight UA921 from London's Heathrow Airport to Dulles Airport in Washington, D.C. The second departure was N766UA, flying as Flight UA921 from Denver to Dulles. This flight was actually the first arrival, touching

In March 1996, Hong Kong's Cathay Pacific was the first airline to take delivery of a 777 powered by the Rolls-Royce RB211 Trent high-bypass turbofan engine. Registered as N77772, the 777-267 aircraft had first operated with the engines in May 1995, and had flown in United States registry during the engine certification process before being turned over to Cathay Pacific as B-HNA.

down just ahead of N777UA. The third departure was N767UA, flying as Flight UA940 from Frankfurt to Chicago's O'Hare International Airport. Flight UA940 touched down at 12:06 P.M. CDT, 20 minutes ahead of schedule. Less than a week later, on June 11, Boeing flew the 777 from Seattle to the Paris Air Show at Le Bourget Airport in nine hours and two minutes, establishing yet another jetliner speed record.

## Subtype Designations

When referencing a commercial jetliner, it is typical to call it by the shortest version of its model number. We refer to a Boeing 747 as simply a "Boeing 747," although any 747 is more than a 747. There have been four distinctive subtypes of the 747, each of them identified with a three-digit suffix. (By comparison, the subtype suffixes that were used by the Douglas component of McDonnell Douglas had two-digit suffixes that performed exactly the same function.)

The original 747 type was the 747-100, which entered commercial service in 1970. The nearly identical 747-200, with increased payload capacity, entered service a year later, and the two remained in production simultaneously for more than a decade. The 747-300, which went into service in 1983, was distinguished from earlier 747s by its extended upper deck and increased passenger capacity. The 747-400, first delivered in 1989, had an extended upper deck (like that of the 747-300) as well as six-foot "winglets" on the wing tips and improved overall performance. (The 747-400 is the only 747 in production since 1990, although discussions of possible 747-500 and 747-600 variants are ongoing.)

The 737-100 was introduced in the 1960s. Three decades later, the series had worked its way up to 737-900. The 737 type was Boeing's best-selling commercial aircraft and the best-selling jet in the company's history.

Beginning with the introduction of the 757 and 767, Boeing adopted the practice of bypassing the "-100" variant, and essentially delivering no aircraft that is less than "-200" standard in order to signify that the aircraft had passed from flight test to operational status. As such, the first aircraft delivered were a 757-200 and a 767-200.

The same would be true with the 777. The first of the series to go into service in June 1995 were "777-200 type" aircraft. Actually, they weren't *literally* 777-200s. The suffix is always further modified to reflect the airline customer's two digit code. For United Airlines, the code is "22," so the first 777-200s in service were actually 777-222s. The second customer to receive 777-200s was British Airways. Its code was "36," so the aircraft was delivered as 777-236s. Boeing typically refers to them generically under the umbrella designation of 777-200.

Even as the 777-200 was entering service, Boeing was working on the first major subvariant, the 777-200ER, the initials standing for "Extended Range." Assembly of the first 777-200ER began at Everett on February 20, 1996, less than a month after the 25th 777-200 was completed at the factory. The rollout ceremonies for the first 777-200ER were held on September 3, and the aircraft entered scheduled service with British Airways—as a 777-236ER—on February 9, 1997. On April 2, 1997, the extended range of the 777-200ER was showcased when the aircraft set a new "Great Circle Distance Without Landing" record of 12,455.34 miles between Seattle and Kuala Lumpur, Malaysia.

# PASSENGER ELECTRONICS

Among the features that passengers had come to expect at the turn of the twenty-first century were personal electronics. Inflight movies had been a routine part of air travel since the early 1960s, and air-to-ground telephones for use at passenger seats had been added as a regular amenity in the 1980s.

By the 1990s, however, the field of personal electronics had begun to expand rapidly. Individual passengers had long been able to watch the movie or select from several audio channels, but the digital revolution was rapidly expanding the horizons of the seated passenger. Carriers such as Britain's Virgin Atlantic had added video consoles with tiny liquid crystal display (LCD) screens at every seat of their 747s, allowing passengers individually to choose from several movies or play video games.

In 1995 the 777 was the first aircraft type designed from the outset to be equipped with personal electronics. Introduced on the 777's first day of operation, the United Airlines Interactive Video System (IVS) was touted as the most technologically advanced in-flight entertainment, information, and communications system on the market. The IVS featured LCD color monitors at every seat, six concurrent video channels, up to 19 channels of compact disc-quality audio programming, and air-to-ground/ground-to-air phone links. The communications information for the IVS was directed to cabin nodes, where National Semiconductor High-Performance DP83032 SONIC and DP83950 RIC Ethernet networking chips directed the flow of information to individual passenger seats.

## The 777-300

The next major series variant would be the 777-300. In terms of its marketing hook, it was envisioned as an aircraft that offered virtually the same passenger capacity and range capability as the 747-100 and 747-200 of the 1970s—while burning a third less fuel and having 40 percent lower maintenance costs.

The 777-300 was very much a market-driven aircraft. Boeing was targeting the same demographics that it had two decades earlier—offering the same performance wrapped in a newer package with lower operating costs.

In terms of its range capability, the 777-300 was designed to serve routes of more than 6,700 miles, such as those between Tokyo and Singapore, Honolulu and Seoul, San Francisco and Paris, or San Francisco and Tokyo. As such, it would be a direct competitor with the Airbus Industrie A330 and A340.

The Boeing board of directors formally authorized development of the 777-300 in time for CEO Frank Shrontz to formally announce the aircraft at the Paris Air Show on June 26, 1995. It had been less than three weeks since the basic 777-200 went into service.

A light January snow lay on the ground at Paine Field in Everett in 1996 when Sirius, the first 777-246 to wear the "Red Crane" logo of Japan Airlines, made its debut flight. The Japanese flag carrier had decided to call its 777 fleet "Star Jets" and had adopted the practice of naming each of them after a major star or constellation. The star Sirius is, of course, the second brightest star in the sky after the sun.

The 777-300 was a very pre-planned and market-driven aircraft. In fact, the green light signaled by Frank Schrontz at Paris came in conjunction with formal 777 announcements from four Asian airlines—All Nippon Airways, Cathay Pacific Airways, Korean Air, and Thai Airways International. They announced that, between them, they intended to order a total of 31 777-300s, valued at approximately $3.1 billion. Later in the year, Japan Airlines placed an order for five 777-300s, and Malaysia Airlines soon followed with orders of its own in January 1996.

The 777-300 would be a "stretched" or lengthened variation of the 777-200. Under the "Design for Growth" doctrine, jetliners inevitably are stretched. As had been the case with Boeing and Douglas aircraft dating back to the 707 and DC-8, the huge 777 was conceived with the knowledge that an even larger variant would come after it. Indeed, Boeing had been studying the market feasibility of stretching the 777-200 for some time.

As with the original 777 program in the early 1990s, more than a dozen airlines were involved in working groups to establish customer requirements and firm up aspects of the design for the proposed stretch. Of course, the 777-300 was not an afterthought. Boeing had been thinking ahead, and the 777 facility at Everett had been prepared since 1990 for an aircraft the size of the 777-300.

The 777-300 was stretched to 242 feet 3 inches from the 777-200's 209 feet 1 inch. This made the 777-300 the longest jetliner in the world—ten feet five inches longer than a 747-400!

Passenger capacity for the 777-300 would be 386 in a typical three-class configuration or up to 550 in an all-economy configuration, compared to between 305 and 440 for the 777-200 in similar configurations.

Below deck, the 777-300's hold was designed to accommodate 44 standard LD-3 containers—compared to 32 for its smaller sister ship—as well as provide the same 600 cubic feet of space for bulk cargo. The total lower-hold volume would be 7,080 cubic feet, compared to just over 5,300 cubic feet for the 777-200.

The baseline maximum takeoff weight for the 777-300 would be 580,000 pounds, with the highest maximum takeoff weight being 660,000 pounds. The fuel capacity for the basic 777-200 was 31,000 gallons, while the 777-200ER and the 777-300 could carry up to 45,220 gallons.

On April 7, 1997, assembly got underway on the first 777-300, as crews at Everett loaded the first 105-foot wing spar into the tool

In June 1996, All Nippon Airways (ANA) took delivery of JA8189, the 25th 777-type aircraft delivered to Japan's second-largest carrier. ANA had been one of the original airlines in the "Working Together" partnership that provided input during the development of the 777 series. The ANA fleet was a mix of 777-281s and 777-281ER "Extended Range" jetliners.

RIGHT
The first 777-289 delivered to Japan Air System was also touted as being the first aircraft to offer three classes of service on Japanese domestic routes. The carrier would use the seven ships of its initial order on high-density routes connecting Tokyo with Fukuoka in the south and Sapporo in the north. The "rainbow ribbon" livery had been selected from 10,461 designs submitted during a contest held over the Internet.

that automatically drills, measures, and installs fasteners—more than 5,000 of them. By this time, seven Asian airlines—All Nippon Airways, Cathay Pacific Airways, Korean Air, Thai Airways International, Malaysia Airlines, Japan Airlines, and Asiana Airlines—had ordered 50 777-300 aircraft. Meanwhile, order books contained a total of 323 orders for 777s of both the -200 and -300 variants.

With two Japanese carriers having placed orders, it is important to point out that Boeing's Japanese industrial partners—through the Japanese Aircraft Development Corporation (JADC)—were as much involved in the 777-300 as they had

On March 21, 1997, following his prepared text, Korean Air President Yang Ho Cho said, "We are delighted to have this award-winning Boeing jetliner become part of our fleet." He was referring to HL7530, the first 777-285ER to be delivered to his company.

been in the 777-200. The first Japanese-built structural parts for the 777-300 were wing in-spar ribs that were designed and built by Japan Aircraft Manufacturing, Ltd. These were unloaded at Everett on May 9, 1997. In turn, forward body panels built by Kawasaki arrived on May 20, aft body panels from Mitsubishi reached Everett on May 27, the wing center section made by Fuji came in on May 30, and the wing-to-body fairings manufactured by Shin Miwa arrived on July 8.

The rollout of the first 777-300 was celebrated exactly two months later, on September 8, just one day before the Boeing Commercial Airplane Group celebrated the completion of the 100th airframe of the 777 program. The first flight of the 777-300,

lasting four hours and six minutes, came on October 16, 1997. On May 4, 1998, after a six-month flight-test program, the 777-300 became the first commercial aircraft in history to receive both its type certification and its 180-minute ETOPS certification from both the American FAA and the European JAA on the same day. The first 777-300 was delivered to Cathay Pacific Airways in June 1998.

### Staged Engine Introduction

The complexity of introducing a new commercial aircraft is magnified when the plane is offered with a choice of engines and a choice of variants. Each of the variants requires testing, and so

Catching the last rays of an April setting sun as it maneuvers over the Pacific, 9M-MRA, a 777-2H6ER Extended Range, was the first 777 delivered to the national flag carrier of Malaysia. The "50" inscribed on the aft fuselage of 9M-MRA was in celebration of the fiftieth anniversary of the airline in 1997.

do the Engines. Three distinct aircraft types—777-200, 777-300 and 777-200ER—as well as three engine choices means that there would be nine distinct 777s within the first several years of operation. The engines that were offered provided a wide range of thrust ratings. The first generation ranged from 74,000 to 77,200 pounds, roughly 60 percent greater than the rating of the engine class that first equipped the 767. Subsequent variations of the families of engines produced by the three engine-makers would boast thrust ratings up to and exceeding 100,000 pounds.

The first engine type, the Pratt & Whitney, was put into service along with the first 777 airframe on June 7, 1995. The second of the engine choices, the General Electric option, first entered service on a British Airways 777-236 on November 11 of the same year. The Rolls-Royce Trent followed, aboard a Cathay Pacific 777-267, on March 31, 1996.

The Pratt & Whitney PW4000 series high-bypass turbofan engines used on the 777 have a fan tip diameter of 112 inches—only three feet narrower than the fuselage of a Boeing 737. The 112 inches compare to the 78.5-inch diameter of the PW2000 series that is specified for the Boeing 757, or the 93.4 inches of the Pratt & Whitney JT9D family that was used for both the 747 and 767 programs. The PW4000 series also includes a family of 94-inch engines that are used on the 767-300 and 747-400, as well as a 100-inch engine used by the Airbus A330.

A solid, long-time customer for large Boeing jetliners, Singapore Airlines received its first 777-212 in May 1997. It had been dubbed Jubilee in celebration of the carrier's 50th anniversary that year. In November 1995, Singapore had placed 34 firm orders for 777 aircraft—plus options for another 43. The total value in current dollars was $12.7 billion. Through September 2001, the airline had received 26 of these. Most were 777-212ERs, but a half dozen were 777-312s.

Emirates Airways, the flag carrier of the United Arab Emirates, ordered and received a total of nine 777-21H aircraft, all but three of which were 777-21HER Extended Range ships. The latter are powered by Rolls-Royce RB211 Trent high-bypass turbofans and were configured at Everett to carry 303 passengers.

Taking off from Paine Field under wet runway conditions seldom experienced at home, this Egypt Air 777-277ER was the first of three of its kind delivered to the Egyptian national flag carrier. All were powered with Pratt & Whitney PW4000 series high-bypass turbofan engines.

Manufactured with hollow titanium shroudless fan blades, the PW4000 is noted for high efficiency and low noise, along with high resistance to foreign object damage (FOD). As had been the case with the 777 itself, the PW4000 was the first engine to enter service already pre-approved for 180-minute ETOPS.

The original PW4000 series engines used on the 777-200 were of the 77,200-pound-thrust PW4077 subtype, but since the turn of the century, 777-200s and 777-300s have been delivered with the PW4084, PW4090, or PW4098 engines. The latter two digits indicate the engine thrust in thousands of pounds. With 98,000 pounds of thrust, the PW4098 is standard equipment for the 777-300. When it was introduced in August 1999, it was the most powerful commercial engine in the world.

Originally introduced in January 1995 and first flight-tested on a 777 a month later, the General Electric GE90 series is a 124-inch high-bypass turbofan designed specifically for the 777 program. It was certified in November 1995, and went on to receive its 180-minute ETOPS certification in October 1996, and a 207-minute certification in June 2000. The original engines in the series had a thrust rating of 76,000 pounds, but the newer GE90-115B—designed for the 777-300—delivers 115,400 pounds of thrust. At the time that it was introduced in 2000, the GE90-115B was the world's most powerful commercial turbofan engine.

As had been the case with the 777 itself, the GE90 had been created with the input of international partners. General Electric Aircraft Engines had previously developed the extremely successful CFM56 turbofan engine in partnership with France's SNECMA. In the case of the GE90, SNECMA had a 23.5 percent share of the program, compared to 60.5 percent for General Electric. Other international partners were IHI of Japan, with nine percent, and FiatAvio of Italy, with seven percent.

The Rolls-Royce Trent 800-series turbofans were designed specifically for the 777, but are similar to the Trent 700 family seen in service with both the Boeing 747 and Airbus A330 aircraft. The engine has a three-shaft configuration and a second-generation hollow titanium wide-chord fan with a tip diameter of 110 inches. The subtypes deliver between 75,000 and 95,000 pounds of thrust. In the designation numbers, the latter two digits indicate the thrust in thousands of pounds.

The Trent 875, 877, and 884 engines were introduced in 1996 and 1997 for the 777-200, while the Trent 892 was first offered in 1997 for either the 777-200 or 777-300. A Trent 895, introduced in 2000, is likewise available for both 777 variants. The Trent family is estimated to have a "thrust growth capability" of up to 104,000 pounds.

## Evolving Production

At the time of the first flight of the first 777 in June 1994, several additional 777 airframes were already nearing completion at Everett, and within a few months a half dozen had made their first flights. Boeing had 134 orders for 777s by the end of June 1994, including 34 from United Airlines with an option on an

This Thai Airways International (THAI) 777-2D7, registered as HS-TJG, was the 100th 777 to be delivered. It was handed over to THAI in October 1997, 28 months after the first 777 was delivered to United Airlines. Over the next 28 months, 123 777s would be delivered to customers. At the time of the disaster of September 11, 2001, the total number of deliveries had reached 358 against a total of 581 orders.

additional 34. By the end of 1994, a total of 13 777s had rolled out, although there had been no new orders during the second half of the year.

During the first half of 1995, there were 26 orders for 777s, including an order for 23 that was placed by Saudi Arabian Airlines on June 18, shortly after the first 777 had entered service with United Airlines. However, orders picked up briskly after the 777 became operational, and during the first year that the jetliner was in revenue service, Boeing received 123 orders, including orders for 30 aircraft on December 22, 1995.

Two months later, on February 26, 1996, the Boeing Board of Directors announced that Boeing CEO Frank Shrontz would be succeeded by Phil Condit, the executive vice president of Boeing Commercial Airplane Group and, more importantly, the erstwhile general manager of Boeing's 777 Division.

Production stepped up as well. After delivering 13 airframes during the first year, the Boeing Commercial Airplane Group delivered 32 in 1995, 59 in 1997, and 74 in 1998. It was in August of 1998 that the Everett facility implemented its "three-day, one-bay" production model, in which one aircraft

British Airways took delivery of its 25th 777 on June 2, 1999, and had the aircraft in service by the end of the month. Registered as G-VIIU, the aircraft was also the 20th 777-236ER "Extended Range" aircraft that was delivered to the United Kingdom flag carrier. Bob Ayling, the CEO of British Airways, remarked at the time that the 777-236ER was "a centerpiece of our operation as we fly into a new millennium."

rolled out the factory every three manufacturing days, using a single production line or bay.

During 1999, 777 production reached its peak, with a total of 85 airframes. This represented roughly one every 110 hours. On two occasions during the year, on August 12 and December 9, three aircraft would be delivered on a single day.

After a total of 88 orders in 1995 and 79 during 1996, the 777 reached its peak year for orders with 117 in 2000. These years are recalled as also being the peak of one of the airline industry's periodic booms. As is usually the case, that boom presaged the inevitable trough that would pinch the industry in the early twenty-first century.

RIGHT
In July 1997, Boeing Commercial Airplane Group mechanics at Everett joined the three major fuselage sections of the first 777-300 aircraft. This would also be the fifth of the 777 series to be delivered to Hong Kong's Cathay Pacific Airways, which had previously taken four 777-200s. The big aircraft would be 33 feet 3 inches longer than the 777-200.

The first Boeing 777-300, seen here with a THAI 777-200 in the background, nears final assembly on the floor at Everett in September 1997. Next, the engines will be hung and the auxiliary power unit (APU) will be installed. This is the point on the assembly line where the interiors typically are installed, but since this aircraft was the first of a derivative model, Boeing would be installing flight-test equipment.

An interesting item in the orders for 777s in 2000 was a total of 48 aircraft ordered by two major leasing companies, General Electric Capital and International Lease Finance. Also notable that year were the 14 ordered by Air France, an airline that typically favors French-manufactured Airbus equipment. This may or may not have had something to do with a passenger preference survey released in June 1999 showing that three out of four passengers who had flown on both the Boeing 777 and the Airbus A330/A340 preferred the 777. Six airlines had conducted the survey, canvassing nearly 6,000 passengers who had flown in both aircraft types.

By now, discerning passengers would have had firsthand experience with the cabin interiors and the practical effect of some facts and figures that had been made available to airline representatives visiting the cabin mockup at Renton during the early 1990s. In economy class, 18.5-inch-wide seats were standard in the 777, compared to 17.2-inch seats on the Airbus jetliners. Another advantage of the 777 was the amount of space between the heads of passengers seated in window seats and the cabin sidewall. With 10.75 inches aboard the 777, passengers perceived the sidewall as being nearly straight. By contrast, A340 passengers had only 5.22 inches between their heads and the sidewall.

In 2001 orders dropped to just 18, the lowest number since the aircraft had gone into service. The reason was more the global economic downturn than the terrorist attacks that crippled the airline industry during the fourth quarter. Although there were no more orders in 2001 after the September 11 tragedy, the 777 program did not suffer from the surge of cancellations that impacted other Boeing programs, especially the 757 program. Deliveries for 2001 were actually up from those of the previous year, increasing modestly from 55 to 58 aircraft.

At the end of 2001—an extremely difficult year—Boeing had delivered 374 777 aircraft against orders for 581. Of those that had been delivered, 336 were 777-200s. The largest customer for

The first Boeing 777-300 was rolled out on September 8, 1997, at a ceremony held at the Commercial Airplane Group facility at Everett. Several hundred airline customer employees joined the thousands of Boeing workers who turned out to celebrate. After flight testing, this 777-300 would be delivered to Cathay Pacific Airways of Hong Kong in May 1998.

the 777 was the launch customer, United Airlines, with 54 aircraft in service out of 61 ordered in five separate orders between 1990 and 1998. The second largest customer was British Airways, which was then operating all 45 aircraft that it had ordered. American Airlines, the largest U.S. carrier, was a close third, then operating 39 out of 47 aircraft that it had ordered through the end of 2000. The largest operator outside Europe and the United States was Saudi Arabian Airlines, then flying a fleet of 23 777s.

In Japan, where Boeing's industrial partners had contributed to the development of the 777, the numbers were lower than had been originally projected because of the economic downturn that Japan suffered during the 1990s. All Nippon Airways was the largest 777 operator in Japan, with 21 aircraft, followed by Japan Airlines with ten and Japan Air System with seven.

## Marketing the Longer-Range Derivatives Program

As had happened numerous times throughout the half-century history of Boeing Commercial Airplane Group jetliner programs, the company began the twenty-first century by studying market niches for which there were no aircraft to fill them. From the first 707 through the 777-300, the story of Boeing commercial aircraft had been that of building on past experience to address those needs and niches.

Aircraft types must evolve in order to flourish. A good example, or case study, is the Boeing 737. It has been in production for more than four decades and is continuously refreshed with new variants up to and including the 737-900 and numerous other subvariants, including the Boeing Business Jet (BBJ), which is marketed separately as an executive aircraft. Such longevity—and family building—is and must be part of the market consideration that drives the 777 program.

On June 17, 1999, Boeing announced that it had been studying longer-range derivatives of the 777. Two market segments were to be studied.

First was the market niche related to long routes that could then be served only by the 747-400, but for which there were not enough passengers to fill a huge aircraft like the 747-400. Flying with empty seats was a waste, so there was a need for a smaller aircraft that would have the same range as the 747-400.

Second was the market niche for a jetliner that could fly longer routes than had ever been served routinely before. This comprised routine, nonstop service between such important destination pairings as Singapore and New York, Atlanta and Hong Kong, Sydney and Dallas, or Paris and Taipei.

An important marketing consideration in the development of both the airframe and engine aspects of a longer-range derivative would be fuel economy. The goal was to demonstrate seat-mile costs that would be up to 22 percent lower than the competing A340-500 and A340-600 aircraft. Studies had moved forward quickly enough that on July 6, 1999, three weeks after the program was first officially mentioned, Boeing announced that a derivative of the General Electric GE90 turbofan engine had been chosen to be the sole power plant for the proposed longer-range derivatives. With a nod from the board of directors, the Longer Range Derivatives program was formally launched on February 29, 2000—even as the 250th 777 airframe was entering service. The program would involve both the 777-200 and the 777-300. The new 777-300 would be designated as the 777-300ER (Extended Range). The 777-200 would be called 777-200LR, for "Longer Range," to distinguish it from the 777-200ER "Extended Range" which already existed.

The 777-200LR would be powered by the GE90-110B1, with 110,000 pounds of thrust. The 777-300ER was to be equipped with a pair of GE90-115Bs, delivering 115,000 pounds of thrust. The maximum ranges for fully loaded and fueled aircraft increased from 5,996 miles for the basic 777-200 to 10,138 miles for the 777-200LR, and from 6,853 miles for the 777-300 to 8,257 miles for the 777-300ER.

The 777-200LR was conceived as the longest-ranging aircraft in the world. This would make routine non-stop service possible between the destinations noted above, with an approximate flight time of 18 hours on the longest of these routes.

The 777-300ER would have the same range as the 747-400, but less passenger capacity and lower operational cost (because of smaller size and lower weight). It would be capable of serving routes such as Paris to Los Angeles, Frankfurt to Singapore, Rome to Chicago, New York to Tokyo, or Johannesburg to London.

The debut flight of the first Boeing 777-300 occurred on October 16, 1997. Sporting Rolls-Royce Trent engines, the new aircraft took off from Payne Field at Everett and headed north to the San Juan Islands before turning west across the Strait of Juan de Fuca to the Olympic Peninsula. The 777-300 is seen here over the snow-frosted peaks of the Olympic Range.

The first order, for eight 777-300ERs, came from Japan Airlines on March 31, 2000. On June 27, EVA Air ordered three 777-200LRs and four 777-300ERs. All Nippon Airways ordered six 777-300ERs on July 18, and Air France ordered 10 777-300ERs in November.

New engineering and structural changes would make the Longer Range Derivative airframes approximately 35 percent different from existing 777 airframes. The wings would be extended by about 6.5 feet on both sides with the addition of raked wing-tips. This would also enhance fuel capacity. Provisions for up to three optional fuel tanks were also included in the aft cargo compartment of the 777-200LR. The fuselage, wing, empennage, and nose gear of the aircraft would be strengthened and new main landing gear would be used. New wheels, tires, and brakes would be developed.

ABOVE
An early 777-300 with Pratt & Whitney PW4098 high-bypass turbofan engines is seen here during the 1,400 hours of flight testing that occurred with the type. These hours were logged between October 1997 and May 1998, when the first 777-300 was delivered to Cathay Pacific Airways of Hong Kong.

Japanese Taiko drummers hard at work at Paine Field in Everett. Ethnic music and dance is occasionally part of the festivities when Boeing makes a milestone delivery. Such was the case in June 1998, when All Nippon Airways (ANA) received its first 777-381. Through 2001, ANA would take delivery of five 777-381s, as well as four 777-281ERs and a dozen 777-281s.

PREVIOUS PAGES
In September 1998, Boeing used this Thai Airways International (THAI) 777 to showcase the 300-series 777s at the Farnborough Air Show in the United Kingdom. This aircraft, the first of the series to be operated by THAI, was powered by Rolls-Royce RS892 Trent high-bypass turbofan engines.

The first 777-300 series aircraft to be delivered was this 777-367 that was handed over to Hong Kong's Cathay Pacific on May 21, 1998. According to Peter Sutch, the chairman of Cathay's parent, the Swire Group, the 300-series was envisioned as "the high-capacity workhorse for our short-haul Asian regional network." Although both Sutch and Boeing Chairman Phil Condit were present that day, all eyes were on the lovely Chinese dancers—and the beautiful 777-367.

RIGHT
Given the name Anacreon, JA751A was the first All Nippon Airways (ANA) 777-381. Although most ANA jetliners get Japanese names, this ship's namesake was a Greek lyric poet who lived from about 570 to 485 B.C. at Samos and at Athens, where his patron was Hipparchus. His poetry celebrates the joys of wine and love and inspired a genre of poems called Anacreontics that were penned in his style from Hellenistic to late Byzantine times. A few millennia later, the bard would have added the joys of 777 travel to his repertoire.

The significantly higher-thrust engines would require revisions in the struts and nacelles.

One of the most interesting and advanced features in the Longer Range Derivatives program would be the supplementary electronic tailskid, which would become standard on both the 777-200LR and the 777-300ER. Actually, it was not really a tailskid at all, but a very sophisticated sensor. Like a real tailskid, this "virtual" software feature would act to help prevent inadvertent scraping of the tail on the runway at takeoff or landing. It would, in turn, "command" elevator movement if the aircraft's attitude exceeded preset limits and the tail was about to impact the pavement.

With extended range and extended flight times, engineers were given the task of augmenting crew and attendant rest stations. In rethinking this issue conceptually, it was decided to move these quarters off the main deck. This would give the crews the added comfort and restfulness of separate quarters for breaks during long flights. In light of the September 11, 2001, hijackings, this move would also add to the potential of enhanced security for crewmembers during a siege. Finally, by moving crew and attendant quarters off the main deck, airlines could free up space to add as many as 14 revenue seats. As had been the case for half a century, jetliner development came down to whatever pleased the airline customers, and that which pleases them most is filled revenue seats.

Japan Airlines received its first 777-346, registered as JA8941, in October 1998. Following the practice of naming its 777 fleet after stars and constellations, the airline dubbed this ship Regulus, the brightest star in the Constellation Leo. Through 2001, the carrier would take delivery of ten 777 series aircraft, equally divided between 777-246s and 77-346s.

117

# APPENDIX A

## Technical Specifications: 777-200

Range: 5,996 miles (9,650 kilometers)

Cruising Speed at 35,000 feet (10,668 meters): Mach 0.84 (620 miles per hour/1,000 kilometers per hour)

Wing Span: 199 feet 11 inches (60.9 meters)
Length: 209 feet 1 inch (63.7 meters)
Tail Height: 60 feet 9 inches (18.5 meters)
Interior Cabin Width: 19 feet 3 inches (5.86 meters)
Diameter: 20 feet 4 inches (6.19 meters)

Passenger Capacity:
Three-class configuration: 305
Two-class configuration: 400
Single-class configuration: Up to 440

Cargo Capacity:
Total volume: 5,302 cubic feet (150.2 cubic meters) including up to six pallets or 14 LD-3 containers, plus 600 cubic feet (17 cubic meters) of bulk cargo

Engines at maximum thrust:
Pratt & Whitney PW4077 (77,000 pounds, 34,927 kilograms)
Rolls-Royce Trent 877 (76,000 pounds, 34,474 kilograms)
General Electric GE90-77B (77,000 pounds, 34,927 kilograms)

Maximum Fuel Capacity: 31,000 gallons (117,348 liters)

Maximum Takeoff Weight:
545,000 pounds (247,212 kilograms)

# APPENDIX B

## Technical Specifications: 777-200ER

Range: 8,896 miles (14,316 kilometers)

Cruising Speed at 35,000 feet (10,668 meters): Mach 0.84 (620 miles per hour/1,000 kilometers per hour)

Wing Span: 199 feet 11 inches (60.9 meters)
Length: 209 feet 1 inch (63.7 meters)
Tail Height: 60 feet 9 inches (18.5 meters)
Interior Cabin Width: 19 feet 3 inches (5.86 meters)
Diameter: 20 feet 4 inches (6.19 meters)

Passenger Capacity:
Three-class configuration: 301
Two-class configuration: 400
Single-class configuration: Up to 440

Cargo Capacity:
Total volume: 5,302 cubic feet (150.2 cubic meters) including up to six pallets or 14 LD-3 containers, plus 600 cubic feet (17 cubic meters) of bulk cargo

Engines at maximum thrust:
Pratt & Whitney PW4090 (90,000 pounds, 40,824 kilograms)
Rolls-Royce Trent 895 (93,400 pounds, 42,366 kilograms)
General Electric 90-94B (93,700 pounds, 42,502 kilograms)

Maximum Fuel Capacity: 45,220 gallons (171,160 liters)

Maximum Takeoff Weight: 656,000 pounds (297,560 kilograms)

# APPENDIX C

## Technical Specifications: 777-200LR

Range: 10,138 miles (16,316 kilometers)

Cruising Speed at 35,000 feet (10,668 meters): Mach 0.84 (620 miles per hour/1,000 kilometers per hour)

Wing Span: 212 feet 7 inches (64.8 meters)
Length: 209 feet 1 inch (63.7 meters)
Tail Height: 60 feet 11.5 inches (18.6 meters)
Interior Cabin Width: 19 feet 3 inches (5.86 meters)
Diameter: 20 feet 4 inches (6.19 meters)

Passenger Capacity:
Three-class configuration: 301 in seating ranges from six-abreast to ten-abreast with two aisles

Cargo Capacity:
Total volume: 5,302 cubic feet (150.2 cubic meters) including up to six pallets or 14 LD-3 containers (or up to three optional body fuel tanks each replacing two LD-3s)

Engines at maximum thrust:
GE90-110B1 (110,100 pounds, 49,941 kilograms)

Maximum Fuel Capacity: 47,890 gallons (181,280 liters)

Maximum Takeoff Weight: 750,000 pounds (340,194 kilograms) with higher gross weights available

# APPENDIX D

## Technical Specifications: 777-300

Range: 6,853 miles (11,029 kilometers)

Cruising Speed at 35,000 feet (10,668 meters): Mach 0.84 (620 miles per hour/1,000 kilometers per hour)

Wing Span: 199 feet 11 inches (60.9 meters)
Length: 242 feet 4 inches (73.9 meters)
Tail Height: 60 feet 8 inches (18.5 meters)
Interior Cabin Width: 19 feet 3 inches (5.86 meters)
Diameter: 20 feet 4 inches (6.19 meters)

Passenger Capacity:
Three-class configuration: 368
Two-class configuration: 451
Single-class configuration: Up to 550

Cargo Capacity:
Total volume: 7,080 cubic feet (200.5 cubic meters) including eight 96x125-inch pallets, 20 LD-3 containers in the aft lower hold, and 600 cubic feet (17 cubic meters) of bulk cargo

Engines at maximum thrust:
Pratt & Whitney PW4098 (97,900 pounds, 44,407 kilograms)
Rolls-Royce Trent 892 (90,000 pounds, 40,824 kilograms)

Maximum Fuel Capacity: 45,220 gallons (171,160 liters)

Maximum Takeoff Weight: 660,000 pounds (299,370 kilograms)

# APPENDIX E

## Technical Specifications: 777-300ER

Range: 8,257 miles (13,288 kilometers)

Cruising Speed at 35,000 feet (10,668 meters): Mach 0.84 (620 miles per hour/1,000 kilometers per hour)

Wing Span: 212 feet 7 inches (64.8 meters)
Length: 242 feet 4 inches (73.9 meters)
Tail Height: 60 feet 11 inches (18.6 meters)
Interior Cabin Width: 19 feet 3 inches (5.86 meters)
Diameter: 20 feet 4 inches (6.19 meters)

Passenger Capacity:
Three-class configuration: 365 in seating ranges from six-abreast to ten-abreast with two aisles

Cargo Capacity:
Total Volume: 7,080 cubic feet (200.5 cubic meters), eight pallets or 20 LD-3 containers (or up to three optional body fuel tanks each replacing two LD-3s)

Engines at maximum thrust:
GE90-115B 115,300 pounds (52,300 kilograms)

Maximum Fuel Capacity: 47,890 gallons (181,280 liters)

Maximum Takeoff Weight: 750,000 pounds (340,194 kilograms) with higher gross weights available

# APPENDIX F

## 777 Deliveries 1995–2001

### 1995 Deliveries

| | |
|---|---|
| May 15: | United Airlines (777-200) |
| May 24: | United Airlines (777-200) |
| May 31: | United Airlines (777-200) |
| June 26: | United Airlines (777-200) |
| June 28: | United Airlines (777-200) |
| July 12: | United Airlines (777-200) |
| September 29: | United Airlines (777-200) |
| October 4: | All Nippon Airways (777-200) |
| November 11: | British Airways (777-200) |
| November 27: | United Airlines (777-200) |
| December 20: | All Nippon Airways (777-200) |
| December 28: | British Airways (777-200) |
| December 28: | China Southern (777-200) |

### 1996 Deliveries

| | |
|---|---|
| January 12: | British Airways (777-200) |
| January 22: | United Airlines (777-200) |
| January 31: | United Airlines (777-200) |
| February 15: | Japan Airlines (777-200) |
| February 29: | China Southern (777-200) |
| March 28: | Japan Airlines (777-200) |
| March 29: | United Airlines (777-200) |
| March 31: | Thai Airways International (777-200) |
| April 11: | United Airlines (777-200) |
| May 9: | Cathay Pacific Airways (777-200) |
| May 20: | British Airways (777-200) |
| May 23: | All Nippon Airways (777-200) |
| June 5: | Emirates (777-200) |
| June 13: | Cathay Pacific Airways (777-200) |
| June 13: | Thai Airways International (777-200) |
| July 3: | Emirates (777-200) |

| | |
|---|---|
| July 18: | United Airlines (777-200) |
| July 26: | United Airlines (777-200) |
| August 6: | United Airlines (777-200) |
| August 12: | All Nippon Airways (777-200) |
| August 14: | All Nippon Airways (777-200) |
| August 23: | Cathay Pacific Airways (777-200) |
| September 12: | Japan Airlines (777-200) |
| September 12: | United Airlines (777-200) |
| October 16: | Emirates (777-200) |
| October 25: | Cathay Pacific Airways (777-200) |
| October 25: | Thai Airways International (777-200) |
| November 15: | China Southern (777-200) |
| December 3: | Japan Air System (777-200) |
| December 5: | China Southern (777-200) |
| December 16: | All Nippon Airways (777-200) |
| December 19: | Thai Airways International (777-200) |

### 1997 Deliveries

| | |
|---|---|
| February 6: | British Airways (777-200ER) |
| February 18: | British Airways (777-200ER) |
| February 27: | British Airways (777-200ER) |
| February 28: | China Southern (777-200ER) |
| March 7: | United Airlines (777-200ER) |
| March 11: | United Airlines (777-200ER) |
| March 18: | British Airways (777-200ER) |
| March 21: | Korean Air (777-200ER) |
| March 28: | British Airways (777-200) |
| March 28: | Korean Air (777-200ER) |
| April 4: | United Airlines (777-200ER) |
| April 9: | British Airways (777-200ER) |
| April 11: | Emirates (777-200ER) |
| April 18: | China Southern (777-200ER) |

| | |
|---|---|
| April 21: | Japan Airlines (777-200) |
| April 23: | Malaysia Airlines (777-200ER) |
| April 29: | United Airlines (777-200ER) |
| May 5: | Singapore Airlines (777-200ER) |
| May 7: | British Airways (777-200ER) |
| May 14: | Japan Airlines (777-200) |
| May 15: | Emirates (777-200ER) |
| May 21: | United Airlines (777-200ER) |
| May 23: | British Airways (777-200ER) |
| May 23: | Egyptair (777-200ER) |
| May 30: | Malaysia Airlines (777-200ER) |
| June 5: | United Airlines (777-200ER) |
| June 10: | British Airways (777-200ER) |
| June 23: | All Nippon Airways (777-200) |
| June 24: | Malaysia Airlines (777-200ER) |
| June 26: | Japan Air System (777-200) |
| June 30: | All Nippon Airways (777-200) |
| July 2: | Egyptair (777-200ER) |
| July 3: | British Airways (777-200ER) |
| July 15: | United Airlines (777-200ER) |
| July 18: | Singapore Airlines (777-200ER) |
| July 25: | Emirates (777-200ER) |
| July 30: | Malaysia Airlines (777-200ER) |
| August 6: | Singapore Airlines (777-200ER) |
| August 7: | Egyptair (777-200ER) |
| August 11: | United Airlines (777-200ER) |
| August 15: | Thai Airways International (777-200) |
| August 21: | All Nippon Airways (777-200) |
| August 28: | United Airlines (777-200ER) (two aircraft) |
| September 11: | Singapore Airlines (777-200ER) |
| September 24: | Lauda Air (777-200ER) |
| September 25: | United Airlines (777-200ER) |
| September 29: | Thai Airways International (777-200) |
| September 30: | Emirates (777-200ER) |
| October 7: | United Airlines (777-200ER) |
| October 31: | Thai Airways International (777-200) |

| | |
|---|---|
| November 18: | United Airlines (777-200ER) |
| November 26: | Japan Air System (777-200) |
| December 9: | United Airlines (777-200ER) |
| December 26: | Saudi Arabian Airlines (777-200ER) |
| December 27: | Saudi Arabian Airlines (777-200ER) |
| December 29: | British Airways (777-200ER) |
| December 29: | Saudi Arabian Airlines (777-200ER) |
| December 30: | Saudi Arabian Airlines (777-200ER) |

**1998 Deliveries**

| | |
|---|---|
| January 8: | International Lease Finance (777-200ER) |
| January 9: | Thai Airways International (777-200) |
| January 12: | International Lease Finance (777-200ER) |
| January 13: | Malaysia Airlines (777-200ER) |
| January 19: | Saudi Arabian Airlines (777-200ER) |
| January 28: | United Airlines (777-200ER) |
| February 3: | British Airways (777-200ER) |
| February 12: | Singapore Airlines (777-200ER) |
| February 13: | International Lease Finance (777-200ER) |
| February 15: | Saudi Arabian Airlines (777-200ER) |
| February 20: | United Airlines (777-200ER) |
| February 28: | United Airlines (777-200ER) |
| March 12: | Singapore Airlines (777-200ER) |
| March 13: | British Airways (777-200ER) |
| March 18: | Malaysia Airlines (777-200ER) |
| March 19: | Saudi Arabian Airlines (777-200ER) |
| March 26: | All Nippon Airways (777-200) |
| March 26: | British Airways (777-200ER) |
| March 27: | Air France (777-200ER) |
| March 30: | Kuwait Airways (777-200ER) |
| April 17: | Saudi Arabian Airlines (777-200ER) |
| April 21: | Air France (777-200ER) |
| April 27: | All Nippon Airways (777-200) |
| April 27: | Japan Air System (777-200) |
| May 5: | Air France (777-200ER) |
| May 8: | United Airlines (777-200ER) |

| | |
|---|---|
| May 15: | Malaysia Airlines (777-200ER) |
| May 20: | All Nippon Airways (777-200) |
| May 22: | Cathay Pacific Airways (777-300) |
| June 11: | Saudi Arabian Airlines (777-200ER) |
| June 12: | Kuwait Airways (777-200ER) |
| June 17: | International Lease Finance (777-200ER) |
| June 18: | Singapore Airlines (777-200ER) |
| June 23: | Japan Air System (777-200) |
| June 25: | Cathay Pacific Airways (777-300) |
| June 27: | Singapore Airlines (777-200ER) |
| June 30: | All Nippon Airways (777-300) |
| July 9: | Singapore Airlines (777-200ER) |
| July 20: | Malaysia Airlines (777-200ER) |
| July 28: | Japan Airlines (777-300) |
| July 29: | All Nippon Airways (777-300) |
| July 31: | Saudi Arabian Airlines (777-200ER) |
| August 7: | Singapore Airlines (777-200ER) |
| August 21: | British Airways (777-200ER) |
| August 26: | Japan Airlines (777-300) |
| August 27: | All Nippon Airways (777-300) |
| September 2: | Japan Air System (777-200) |
| September 17: | Saudi Arabian Airlines (777-200ER) |
| September 23: | Cathay Pacific Airways (777-300) |
| September 28: | Continental Airlines (777-200ER) |
| September 28: | Lauda Air (777-200ER) |
| September 29: | Continental Airlines (777-200ER) |
| October 2: | International Lease Finance (777-200ER) |
| October 20: | All Nippon Airways (777-300) |
| October 20: | Malaysia Airlines (777-200ER) |
| October 26: | Air China (777-200) |
| October 27: | Cathay Pacific Airways (777-300) |
| October 30: | Air China (777-200) |
| October 30: | Emirates (777-200ER) |
| November 10: | Continental Airlines (777-200ER) |
| November 14: | Saudi Arabian Airlines (777-200ER) |
| November 19: | Continental Airlines (777-200ER) |
| November 24: | Air China (777-200) |
| November 24: | Mid East Jet (777-200ER) |
| November 25: | Emirates (777-200ER) |
| December 7: | Continental Airlines (777-200ER) |
| December 8: | Continental Airlines (777-200ER) |
| December 10: | Singapore Airlines (777-300) |
| December 14: | Saudi Arabian Airlines (777-200ER) |
| December 17: | Saudi Arabian Airlines (777-200ER) |
| December 17: | Singapore Airlines (777-300) |
| December 23: | Thai Airways International (777-300) |
| December 29: | Korean Air (777-200ER) |
| December 30: | Thai Airways International (777-300) |

## 1999 Deliveries

| | |
|---|---|
| January 12: | Air France (777-200ER) |
| January 14: | Singapore Airlines (777-300) |
| January 19: | Air France (777-200ER) |
| January 21: | American Airlines (777-200ER) |
| January 26: | British Airways (777-200ER) |
| January 28: | Singapore Airlines (777-300) |
| January 29: | American Airlines (777-200ER) |
| January 29: | Saudi Arabian Airlines (777-200ER) |
| February 3: | United Airlines (777-200ER) |
| February 9: | British Airways (777-200ER) |
| February 17: | Japan Airlines (777-300) |
| February 18: | Continental Airlines (777-200ER) |
| February 19: | International Lease Finance (777-200ER) |
| March 1: | American Airlines (777-200ER) |
| March 1: | Continental Airlines (777-200ER) |
| March 8: | American Airlines (777-200ER) |
| March 11: | Air France (777-200ER) |
| March 18: | British Airways (777-200ER) |
| March 22: | United Airlines (777-200ER) |
| March 23: | Delta Air Lines (777-200ER) |
| March 25: | Cathay Pacific Airways (777-300) |
| March 25: | Saudi Arabian Airlines (777-200ER) |

March 29:  Delta Air Lines (777-200ER)
April 1:  British Airways (777-200ER)
April 6:  All Nippon Airways (777-300)
April 12:  American Airlines (777-200ER)
April 20:  American Airlines (777-200ER)
April 21:  Continental Airlines (777-200ER)
April 22:  Japan Airlines (777-300)
April 30:  Air China (777-200)
May 13:  Japan Air System (777-200)
May 18:  American Airlines (777-200ER)
May 18:  United Airlines (777-200ER)
May 21:  International Lease Finance (777-200ER)
May 25:  American Airlines (777-200ER)
May 26:  British Airways (777-200ER)
May 27:  Continental Airlines (777-200ER)
May 28:  British Airways (777-200ER)
June 21:  American Airlines (777-200ER)
June 22:  Malaysia Airlines (777-200ER)
June 24:  Cathay Pacific Airways (777-300)
June 24:  Singapore Airlines (777-200ER)
June 27:  American Airlines (777-200ER)
June 29:  British Airways (777-200ER)
June 29:  Continental Airlines (777-200ER)
July 16:  International Lease Finance (777-200ER)
July 21:  United Airlines (777-200ER)
July 26:  Malaysia Airlines (777-200ER)
July 30:  British Airways (777-200ER)
August 4:  Continental Airlines (777-200ER)
August 11:  British Airways (777-200ER)
August 12:  Korean Air (777-300) (two aircraft)
August 12:  Singapore Airlines (777-200ER)
August 17:  Japan Airlines (777-300)
August 26:  Singapore Airlines (777-200ER)
August 30:  Air China (777-200)
September 10:  American Airlines (777-200ER)
September 14:  Continental Airlines (777-200ER)

September 24:  Singapore Airlines (777-300)
September 29:  Cathay Pacific Airways (777-300)
October 6:  All Nippon Airways (777-200ER)
October 8:  International Lease Finance (777-200ER)
October 18:  Thai Airways International (777-300)
October 21:  Continental Airlines (777-200ER)
October 22:  British Airways (777-200ER)
October 22:  Saudi Oger Ltd. (777-200ER)
November 12:  Singapore Aircraft Leasing Enterprise (777-300)
November 12:  United Airlines (777-200ER)
December 6:  Air France (777-200ER)
December 7:  Delta Air Lines (777-200ER)
December 8:  Thai Airways International (777-300)
December 9:  Saudi Arabian Airlines (777-200ER) (three aircraft)
December 10:  Delta Air Lines (777-200ER)
December 13:  Delta Air Lines (777-200ER)
December 16:  United Airlines (777-200ER)
December 17:  Delta Air Lines (777-200ER)
December 21:  Delta Air Lines (777-200ER)
December 22:  Air France (777-200ER)
December 23:  Singapore Aircraft Leasing Enterprise (777-300)
December 28:  Korean Air (777-300)

**2000 Deliveries**

January 7:  British Airways (777-200ER)
January 18:  British Airways (777-200ER)
January 27:  Air France (777-200ER)
January 27:  American Airlines (777-200ER)
January 28:  United Airlines (777-200)
February 4:  British Airways (777-200ER)
February 18:  British Airways (777-200ER)
February 29:  American Airlines (777-200ER)
March 1:  American Airlines (777-200ER)
March 29:  American Airlines (777-200ER)
April 7:  International Lease Finance (777-200ER)

| | |
|---|---|
| April 12: | American Airlines (777-200ER) |
| April 16: | British Airways (777-200ER) |
| April 21: | American Airlines (777-200ER) |
| April 28: | American Airlines (777-200ER) |
| May 5: | International Lease Finance (777-200ER) |
| May 10: | All Nippon Airways (777-200ER) |
| May 17: | British Airways (777-200ER) |
| May 18: | United Airlines (777-200) |
| May 23: | Air China (777-200) |
| May 31: | American Airlines (777-200ER) |
| June 5: | American Airlines (777-200ER) |
| June 15: | All Nippon Airways (777-200ER) |
| June 22: | American Airlines (777-200ER) |
| June 27: | Korean Air (777-300) |
| June 28: | American Airlines (777-200ER) |
| June 30: | Air China (777-200) |
| July 21: | United Airlines (777-200ER) |
| July 28: | United Airlines (777-200) |
| July 31: | American Airlines (777-200ER) |
| August 14: | United Airlines (777-200ER) |
| August 15: | United Airlines (777-200) |
| August 25: | United Airlines (777-200) |
| August 30: | United Airlines (777-200) |
| September 14: | American Airlines (777-200ER) |
| September 26: | International Lease Finance (777-300) |
| September 27: | British Airways (777-200ER) |
| September 30: | Saudi Arabian Airlines (777-200ER) |
| October 3: | All Nippon Airways (777-200ER) |
| October 14: | British Airways (777-200ER) |
| October 17: | Thai Airways International (777-300) |
| October 18: | Korean Air (777-200ER) |
| November 2: | British Airways (777-200ER) |
| November 9: | Korean Air (777-200ER) |
| November 14: | Air France (777-200ER) |
| November 17: | Saudi Arabian Airlines (777-200ER) |
| December 1: | American Airlines (777-200ER) |

| | |
|---|---|
| December 6: | Cathay Pacific Airways (777-200) |
| December 8: | British Airways (777-200ER) (two aircraft) |
| December 9: | Air France (777-200ER) |
| December 9: | Thai Airways International (777-300) |
| December 15: | Air France (777-200ER) |
| December 16: | American Airlines (777-200ER) |
| December 18: | American Airlines (777-200ER) |

**2001 Deliveries**

| | |
|---|---|
| January 10: | United Airlines (777-200ER) |
| January 23: | United Airlines (777-200ER) |
| January 26: | American Airlines (777-200ER) |
| January 29: | El Al Israeli Airlines (777-200ER) |
| February 3: | Air France (777-200ER) |
| February 14: | International Lease Finance (777-200ER) |
| February 16: | American Airlines (777-200ER) |
| February 21: | El Al Israeli Airlines (777-200ER) |
| February 28: | Air France (777-200ER) |
| March 16: | American Airlines (777-200ER) |
| March 20: | Singapore Aircraft Leasing Enterprise (777-200ER) |
| March 21: | International Lease Finance (777-200ER) |
| March 22: | International Lease Finance (777-300) |
| March 22: | Singapore Airlines (777-200ER) |
| March 27: | American Airlines (777-200ER) |
| March 30: | Saudi Arabian Airlines (777-200ER) |
| April 4: | American Airlines (777-200ER) |
| April 11: | El Al Israeli Airlines (777-200ER) |
| April 14: | British Airways (777-200ER) |
| April 24: | Singapore Aircraft Leasing Enterprise (777-200ER) |
| May 3: | Singapore Airlines (777-200ER) |
| May 16: | American Airlines (777-200ER) |
| May 18: | Air China (777-200) |
| May 25: | American Airlines (777-200ER) |
| May 25: | Singapore Airlines (777-200ER) |

| | | | |
|---|---|---|---|
| May 25: | United Airlines (777-200ER) | September 17: | British Airways (777-200ER) |
| May 31: | British Airways (777-200ER) | September 27: | Singapore Airlines (777-300) |
| June 1: | Air China (777-200) | September 28: | Korean Air (777-200ER) |
| June 15: | British Airways (777-200ER) | October 3: | Egyptair (777-200ER) |
| June 18: | American Airlines (777-200ER) | October 9: | Singapore Airlines (777-300) |
| June 22: | United Airlines (777-200ER) | October 18: | Egyptair (777-200ER) |
| June 28: | Singapore Airlines (777-200ER) | October 18: | Singapore Airlines (777-200ER) |
| June 29: | Air China (777-200) | October 19: | International Lease Finance (777-200ER) |
| July 19: | Singapore Airlines (777-200ER) | October 30: | British Airways (777-200ER) |
| July 24: | United Airlines (777-200ER) | November 2: | Air France (777-200ER) |
| July 26: | Singapore Airlines (777-200ER) | November 2: | International Lease Finance (777-200ER) |
| July 27: | American Airlines (777-200ER) | November 6: | American Airlines (777-200ER) |
| August 1: | Saudi Arabian Airlines (777-200ER) | November 13: | American Airlines (777-200ER) |
| August 16: | Singapore Airlines (777-200ER) | November 15: | Singapore Airlines (777-200ER) |
| August 24: | American Airlines (777-200ER) | November 19: | International Lease Finance (777-200ER) |
| August 24: | United Airlines (777-200ER) | November 20: | Singapore Airlines (777-200ER) |
| August 30: | International Lease Finance (777-200ER) | | |